This book is to be returned on
the last date stamped

LIBREX

Teaching Improvised Drama

Teaching Improvised Drama

a handbook for secondary schools

Peter Chilver MA, PhD

B T Batsford Limited *London*

Jacket photographs by Terry Williams

© Peter Chilver 1978

First published 1978

ISBN 0 7134 1036 1

Typeset by Tek Art Ltd
London S.E.20
Printed in Great Britain by
Billing & Sons Ltd
London, Guildford and Worcester
for the publishers
B T Batsford Limited
4 Fitzhardinge Street
London W1H 0AH

Contents

Introduction 9
1 What is drama? 10
2 What is improvised drama? and what is its use? 12
3 What is the educational value of improvised drama? 14
4 What is the place of improvised drama in the curriculum? 17
5 What is the teacher's role? 18
    Setting up the lesson 18
    Organisation 19
    Setting up structured improvisations 22
    Follow-up work 25
    Evaluation 23

1 Cheating 25
News story — Cheating allegations shake West Point military academy 25
The Queen of Spades by Alexander Pushkin 26
Structured improvisation 27

2 Friendship (See also section 21) 30
Sam, the Scrounger 30
Alexander the Great by Plutarch 32
Z Cars: Window Dressing by Roland Eyre 33
Structured improvisation 35

3 Running Away 36
News story — Schoolboy missing from home 36
Out of Bounds by Esmond Romilly 37
News stories — Boy booted out of games; A chimney tomb for
    runaway 38
Structured improvisation 39

4 Espionage (See also section 25) 42
What makes a good spy? 42
The Craft of Intelligence by Allen Dulles 42
The Philby Affair 43
My Silent War by Kim Philby 43
Informers 45
Images of Deviance edited by Stanley Cohen 45
Structured improvisation 46

5 The Big and the Small 48
Geordie by David Walker 48
News story — Bus fare for white mouse 49
Structured improvisation 51

6 Family Life 53
Five Green Bottles by Ray Jenkins 53
A House for Mr Biswas by V S Naipaul 54
News story — Stop the jet — we want to get off! 56
Structured improvisation 56

7 Adventure 59
The Gest of Robin Hood: A medieval ballad 59
News stories — Boy discovers microfilm; 60
  Desert island rescue 62
Folk Devils and Moral Panic by Stanley Cohen 63

8 Thief 65
News story — Two sisters steal from pensioners 65
Moll Flanders by Daniel Defoe 65
Kleptomaniacs 66
Hons and Rebels by Jessica Mitford 67
Structured improvisation 67

9 Telling Tales 70
News story — Schoolboy paid out £234 to blackmailer 70
The folktale 71
The Myth of the Eternal Return by Marcel Eliade 71
Structured improvisation 72

10 The Gang 75
Coming up for Air by George Orwell 75
News story — Gang mugs park boy for 50p 76
Two Worlds of Childhood by Urie Bronfenbremmer 77

11 Lies 80
News story — West Point cadet accused 80
The lie detector 81
Inside the Company by Philip Agee 81

12 Aggression 83
News story — Boy plays truant from bullies 83
Ritualised fights 84
On Aggression by Konrad Lorenz 84
News stories — Violence on TV exhausts children; I will take on boys,
  too 85
For improvisation 86

Contents 7

13 Fame and Fortune 88
News stories — Arsenal snaps up young Brennan; Former champion dies in poverty; Punk Rock stars on the dole 88
Structured improvisation 89

14 Evidence 91
News story — Rewards for children who chased man 91
Mistaken Identity: court evidence from trial of Peter Hain 92
Structured improvisation 96

15 School 98
Understanding Children Talking by Nancy Martin 98

For older students

16 Orders are Orders 100
The Face of the Third Reich by Joachim C Fest 100
The Last Secret by Nicholas Bethell 101
The Charge of the Light Brigade 103
The Destruction of Lord Raglan by Christopher Hibbert 103
Structured improvisation 105

17 Red Tape 108
Parkinson's Law 108
The Law of Delay by C Northcote Parkinson 108
Chinese Red Tape: article by Simon Leys 110
Structured improvisation 111

18 Winning 114
The Dark by John McGahern 114
Gamesmanship by Stephen Potter 115
Structured improvisation 117

19 Learning 119
The Wild Boy of Aveyron by Jean Itard 119
A Burning Fire: BBC Reith Lectures 1976 121

20 Whodunit? 123
Structured improvisation 123

21 Friendship (see also section 2) 129
Preliminary Pages for a Work of Revenge by Brian Moore 129
Master and disciple 130
Brother Animal by Paul Roazen 130
Structured improvisation 131

8   Contents

22 Whose Responsibility? 134
News story — Many children battered   134
The American Prison Business by Jessica Mitford   134
The Poor by George Simmel   135
Are we responsible for our own actions?   136

23 Starting Work   138
Comments from young people   138
Jobs wanted — advertisements   139
Decline and Fall by Evelyn Waugh   140

24 Violence   142
What makes a young thug?   142
How bad are teenage gangs?   143
The Growth of Crime by Leon Radzinowicz and Joan King   144
Violence and the Police   144
The Law and the Police by Paula Bourne and John Eisenberg   145
Invisible violence — case histories   145

25 Espionage (see also section 4)   147
News story — Fourth man in Philby Case   147
Who Spies?   148
The Game of the Foxes by Ladislas Farago   149
Structured improvisation   150

26 Family Groups   152

27 Crime and Punishment   153
A Walk with Alan by Tom Hart   153

28 Folies à Deux   157
News stories — Couple murder child; Woman kept in filthy cellar   157
Imagination and Reality by Charles Rycroft   158
Structured improvisation   159

29 Fraudulent Conversion   162
Structured improvisation — a mock trial   162

30 Communicating Without Words   172
News story — 'No Smiling', order for accused boy   172
Kinesics and Context by Ray Birdwhistell   172

For further reference   175

Introduction

All good teaching practice is rooted in good theory, and this is as true of improvised drama as it is of anything else. Somebody wishing to teach improvised drama and anyone faced with a request that the subject should be taught in their school or their department, will want to ask and to consider various questions. These would probably include:
1 *What is drama?* Is it, for instance, something that does not appear elsewhere in the curriculum? How does it relate, if at all, to anything else? (Some answers to the question are so wide and all-embracing as to suggest that drama is everything.)
2 *What, then, is improvised drama?* and what is the use of it? Apart from those occasions when we deliberately set up improvisations in the classroom, does it have *any* use?
3 In particular, *what is the educational value of improvised drama?* For example, what do we learn from improvised drama that we do not get from scripted drama, as when we read, say, a play by Shakespeare?
4 *Where, then, does improvised drama belong in the school curriculum?* It could quite reasonably be placed within a large number of other subjects. Does it require a specialised drama teacher?
5 Finally, *what is the teacher's role in a lesson in improvised drama?* Headmasters sometimes complain, not unreasonably, that drama lessons are 'sheer anarchy', and many a good teacher has abandoned the use of improvisation because he or she cannot see their own role in such lessons: 'It was such chaos. I didn't know what to do. I didn't know if I should do anything.'

What follows is a modest attempt to *start* answering these various questions. I do not believe there is a simple answer to any of them, or that there will ever be a final one. All debate about the curriculum of schools is bound to be complex, for not only is there jockeying for power and influence between different 'subjects' but also the problems of the society outside the school are as volatile and elusive as the problems within it. In effect, even the most alert and sensitive of institutions are constantly bound to be out of date.

At the same time, a word of caution may be appropriate. The relationship between theory and practice of the school curriculum is a two-way relationship. Good practitioners think out their theoretical position with care and detachment. And the converse is true of the theorist. There is little point in persuading someone that improvised drama (or any other activity) is theoretically valid, unless both of you get down to the slightly different task of looking at what actually happens when children (or adults) improvise. This can be a time-consuming, not to say a frustrating activity, but the teacher who devotes time to observe in detail the goings-on of a session in improvisation is certain to learn a great deal from doing so. Some of the most valuable research has homed in on precisely this issue, and has produced fascinating transcripts of groups and classes at work on dramatic improvisations. And similarly the major developments in the teaching of English over recent years have emanated in various ways from detailed recording of what actually happens when children write, when they discuss a poem, and so on.

1 *What is drama?*
Drama is essentially a form of expression, of the making of meaning. We are all dramatists, and children show very early in their development a clearly dramatic imagination. Indeed the psychiatrist D.W. Winnicott suggested that drama and thought 'start off' together. The first stirrings of individuality come when the baby starts to dramatise his environment. Usually, says Winnicott, he does this by projecting imaginary and dramatic roles onto objects that are near at hand, such as corners of blankets or toys.

Drama is, then, a basic form, and its subject-matter is human interaction. We think dramatically whenever we seek to make some kind of moving picture of people in action with one another. One could say that it is a form of expression we employ whenever we seek to work out what people have done, or are doing, or will do.

Trying to pin down what it is, can be made slightly less difficult by trying to sort out what it is not. It can be distinguished from three other forms: the narrative form, the lyric form, and what I will call, rather awkwardly perhaps, the symposium form. All these forms are concerned with what is fundamentally the same thing: what people do, what they feel, what they experience. So they could be called the forms of social action. They can be represented in some such way as this:

narrative tells a story

drama acts out the story

lyric expresses the inner thoughts and feelings of the individual or individuals involved;

Symposium represents our attempt to detach ourselves from the ebb and flow of experience and to evaluate it. (In its improvised form we usually speak of a symposium as a discussion.)

These are forms which we use in our everyday lives and our everyday thinking. They are also forms which we create in art and (in the case of the symposium) in the social sciences. *Dramatic art* presents us with people interacting in a context of make-believe and play. A work of dramatic art is seldom if ever purely drama. Even if we go back as far as Aeschylus we find an alternation from dramatic sequences in which the action is played out before the audience, to narrative sequences in which the audience is told what has happened offstage.

All of the following can be taken as examples of the dramatic artist at work:
- the operas of Britten and of Verdi
- the ballets of Ashton and of Robbins
- the films of Chaplin and of Antonioni
- the musicals of Sondheim and of Novello
- the make-believe of all-in wrestling, the most popular and enduring of television entertainments.

All of these are in part dramatic, but with the possible exception of all-in wrestling, all of them also move into and out of other forms. (The great set pieces of classical ballet, for instance, are essentially lyric forms, in which the protagonists reveal their feelings for each other; they are not dramatic interactions.) And it is worth noting that only some of them employ the spoken language. And only some of them are literary. The greatest dramatists of the cinema, Chaplin for instance, are impossible to translate into any literary mode.

The same basic experience will lend itself to all four forms. If, for example, we make a synopsis of the plot of *Romeo and Juliet* for, say, a theatre programme, we will create a simple narrative. The play by Shakespeare, the ballet by Prokofiev, the opera by Berlioz, the musical by Bernstein, are chiefly, but exclusively drama. Most of the dances in the ballet, and most of the songs in the musical, and many of the soliloquys in the play, are ventures into the lyric form. And any endeavour to stand back and explore why such tragedies occur and how perhaps they might be avoided in the future, will move towards the form of the symposium. An example of the latter would be Durkheim's sociological classic, *Suicide*.

It is also worth bearing in mind the different ways in which drama may be *presented* (and improvised). We can distinguish for example: *live* presentation by actors on some kind of stage; *radio* broadcast and sound recording; *film* and television screen and video tape; and *dramatic literature*, where the audience, as readers, respond to the drama by creating their own actors in their own imagination. This may be a work actually created for 'live' enactment, such as a play or an opera, or it may be a novel or short story in which the artist deliberately shapes his material for the private imaginings of the reader. Sometimes the novelist does this so successfully that his material translates for stage or screen almost without adaptation. The works of Dickens and Austen, and more recently of Henry James and Ivy Compton-Burnett would be good examples of this.

I have said that dramatic art is essentially make-believe. This is so even though the line between reality and make-believe is often tenuous and difficult. (Is a live enactment on television of family life, by the family concerned, art or life? Or neither?) In general, though, the distinciton is clear: in dramatic art, no responsibility attaches in the real world to the outcome of the events. The actor playing Othello is not prosecuted in the criminal courts for the murder of Desdemona, provided he does not murder the actress playing the part. Children very early on recognise the distinction. They know that play ceases to be play when the other player bursts into real tears, or the imaginary attack on the imaginary stagecoach becomes all too real, and someone gets hurt.

2 What is improvised drama? and what is its use?
Drama is an art form which can be improvised by the actors. They can get together and make up the drama as they go along, taking their cues from each other. There is nothing especially unusual about this. Jazz is improvised music-making, and is also a group activity, an art-form involving a shared creativity. And of course improvised dramatic art has an honourable ancestry, involving not only the *commedia dell' arte* but also the scripted plays of playwrights such as Moliere, who acknowledges that the written words can convey only marginally the wit and humour that his actors were able to bring to them, and add to them. Indeed the link between improvisation and *comedy* is a very strong one. Freud has suggested that the first dramatist was the first person to tell a joke. And Marjorie Hourd notes that children are very willing and able to elaborate, innovate and improvise humorous incidents, and will depart a long way in such cases from any literary text, such as a story, which happens to be their starting point. But they will hold tightly to the script, in an almost ritualistic fashion, once the tone changes to tragedy.

In the professional theatre, and also in television, Mike Leigh has recently done interesting work as the director of improvised plays (such as *Abigail's Party*). He works in a tradition and a method that owes much to the work of Stanislavsky, and, less famously, to the work of Peter Barkworth when he was teaching at the Royal Academy of Dramatic Art in the 1960s.

In answering the question what is the use of improvised dramatic art, we also answer the question what is the use of dramatic art, for when we *use drama* in the real world, we do not act out a script, we improvise one. But our improvisations are not free. They are not like the fantasy-play of a child pretending to himself that he's Buffalo Bill. They are highly structured. And this brings us back to Stanislavsky and company.

Consider, for a moment, the method employed by Mike Leigh. He approaches each actor on the first day of rehearsal and asks them to find a character:

> 'Generally they come up with a list of five or six friends, people they would like to be, and during the first week or two of rehearsal I then work independently with each of the actors until he or she has selected one: these are not acting exercises in which people are supposed to be funny or inventive or amusing — they're a genuine search for characters who are then researched and built into a final script. Characters develop, then relationships, and these I monitor and push towards a dramatic conflict of some kind, so that you get a microcosm of society through improvisation. . . . But as soon as you start talking about improvisation people expect anarchy. . . in fact, only the surface text is flexible.'

In other words, the actors improvise within an ever-clearer structure. And as Mike Leigh rightly stresses, this is not anarchy, it is not free. It is, as I have said, very much a tradition of Stanislavsky's improvisations, where characters are given complex and detailed situations to 'walk into'. It is a method employed at RADA by Peter Barkworth and it is an essentially simple method. Two actors, would-be improvisers, are drawn out of a group. They are told a basic situation in which they will come together with such knowledge about each other's characters as may be appropriate to the drama. They are then given, individually, detailed biographies and specific motivation to carry them into the scene, such that when the actors meet in the improvisation, they know a great deal about their own characters and their private intentions, and do not know any more about the private intentions of the other character than they would in life. The rest of the group will have probably heard all the instructions to both characters, and hence, in watching the drama unfold, experience all the fun (and sense of irony) of an audience at a scripted play — only more so!

Of course, a clever creator of structured improvisations creates chatacters in an interesting cross-current of motives, as when mother is made to worry about her son's behaviour, when it is the daughter she should really be worried about.

This is also, of course, what we do in life. We structure our improvisations so that we shall know quite precisely what our characters are, our motives and our cues for exit and entrance. Occasionally we even fix the script and learn the lines, in which case we have created an elaborate ceremony or ritual. But these rituals are nevertheless real, not make-believe. They have real consequences: Elizabeth becomes Queen. Miss Brown becomes Mrs Smith. Ritual is not synonymous with make-believe, even though in make-believe we may love to engage in ritual.

While we sometimes create the elaborate rituals of a church service, or a coronation, we more commonly create a loose system of conventions to guide our actions. We create structures which permit a variety of interpretation and performance within certain well defined limits. We create these structures so carefully that we can think about them, teach them, rehearse them, report them, and represent them, quite independently of actually performing them. This is because they can be pressed into a form that is entirely meaningful and complete unto itself: this is the form of drama.

Consider, for example, the various characters gathered together in a law court for a criminal trial. They will have variously different dramatic structures in their minds which they will seek to improvise upon one another. And they will be influenced in the devising of these structures by models drawn from a great diversity of experiences: from first-hand experience, looking at previous cases in the courts, for example; from fiction of various kinds, such as looking at plays and films and reading detective stories; and also from that great mass of experience which is neither entirely 'real' nor entirely 'make-believe', and which could be either, and sometimes is both! These may be the popular myths of society in general (the way we fought the Germans, the Hippies, and so on) or the pervasive myths of this particular branch of the society (such as the stories told by father to son about his days of jury-service, or by old barristers to their juniors about the style and technique of the last Lord Chief Justice). Part real and part fiction, these enter so fully into our thinking as to motivate us very decisively in our overt behaviour to one another.

We could say, then, in answer to the question, What is the use of improvised drama? that we use it all the time, that we are all of us, in real life, improvising dramatists.

3 What then, is the specifically educational value of improvised drama? If we accept the idea that we use drama in an improvised form in the everyday world, and that we use it constantly, we do not, merely because of this, have to include it in the school curriculum. Indeed one could argue in the other direction, and say that something so widely used outside school does not have to be further employed within the classroom. Enough is enough.

The argument for its inclusion in the curriculum is simply this: any classroom session in improvised drama that in any way 'gets off the ground' involves people in re-thinking, in one way or another, what they have previously taken for granted. It may further involve them in thinking about it for the first time. More specifically, it involves them in thinking about the basic subject-matter of all drama — human interaction. To improvise a drama, or to look at others improvising, is to formulate a number of ideas about how people behave, what they do, and why they do it. To do this in an educational context is deliberately to invite consideration, re-consideration, play and experiment with the same subject-matter. In effect, it is to ask: Is this how people behave? Is this human motivation? Is this what happens? Is this how it happens? Is life like this? Could it or should it be like this?

We can be a little more specific. Not only is drama, and improvised drama, to do with the ways people treat each other, it is also to do with the various models which, for better or for worse, lead us to treat each other in this way rather than that. When people start improvising (whether children or adults) they take their material from the same three sources as I outlined in the context of the various personnel gathering together in a law court. They improvise on the basis of:

first-hand experience: what has happened to them in the real, everyday world;

experience drawn from the make-believe dramas of movies, television, comics, and so on;

and the popular myths of their particular society, such as 'punk rockers and how to deal with them', the 'permissive society', 'Scotland Yard', or the star of the local soccer team.

They may use this material solemnly, ritualistically, or they may use it facetiously, perhaps sending it up. They may use it 'realistically', in the Brechtian sense of making a definite comment about it and thus detaching themselves from the material itself; or they may use it 'romantically', in the sense of losing themselves in the sheer fun and delight of the improvisation itself. (This latter distinction would roughly correspond to J. L. Moreno's distinction between a socio-drama and a psycho-drama.) But in either event, they are implicitly making certain comments about people as they have experienced them, and because they are doing it in an educational context, with the services of teachers and the time and opportunity to look at a wide range of different material and ideas, they are extending and deepening their knowledge of people and of how they behave.

This means that while children love to play at and improvise their favourite TV characters, for example, the lesson in 'improvised drama' is perhaps the only opportunity not for 'knocking' such influence on the child's mind, but for using it constructively, helping the child to re-think it on a wider canvas of experience. (I try to be a little more specific about the teacher's role in this when I come to the next two questions.) And the same is true of sessions where we draw on experiences from our own lives, or alternatively from the myths of hearsay and rumour and popular legend. In improvisation, we play with all such material, and while so doing, or having done so, we stand back, we compare notes.

For this reason, there is no conflict between scripted drama and improvised drama. It is not a case of excluding the former in order to encourage the latter. To the contrary. The more experience we have of dramatic literature, for instance, or of cinematic drama, or of the novels of Dickens, the more experience we have on which to draw in our thinking about people and in our material for improvisation. J L Moreno has done fascinating work in the use of improvisation as a form of what might be called 'spontaneity therapy', but he arrives (not unnaturally) at the extreme position of deploring all culture that is not spontaneous. The plays of Shakespeare and the music of Beethoven — they all are condemned, for they do not involve either artists or audience in creating for themselves, spontaneously. But Moreno misses the basic fact that our spontaneity, our creativity, thrives on the creativity of others. Their 'creations' become the raw material for our own play and exploration. Of course, we may become inhibited by the grandeur of their achievements and thus unable to 'play'. But there is no need for this. Indeed one of the tasks of the educator is to assure that this does not happen.

I have said that improvised drama *extends* our knowledge. It does not merely consolidate our position, but, if it is to be considered educational, leads us in some way to rethink our position. This is not only because of the presence of the teacher, but also because of the active involvement, whether as fellow actors or as audience, of the rest of the class. Indeed, the child who remains in the audience, who chooses at certain times not to participate actively, will still learn a great deal. He or she sees other people's inprovisations; is shown corners (and sometimes an entire canvas) of other people's worlds and world-views. At a simple level, though an important one, he learns that *other* parents are possessive, nagging, fussing, indifferent, and so on. He tunes in to the continuing debate about what is real and what is not, what is plausible and what is not. He sees this or that notion laughed out of court — it is too absurd to be acceptable: 'No, we can't do that!' He is presented with the fantasies and fears of others, the jokes and the morality. Of course, it does not come neatly wrapped up and appropriately labelled. Nor does it benefit from solemn unwrapping and scrupulous labelling, though one sometimes fears that the censors in our midst will soon decree that teachers do precisely that: 'Now Johnny told a lie in that story, didn't he. So what *ought* to have happened to him in the end?' Or, 'Susie used bad language when she was the shop assistant, didn't she? What would a *good* shop assistant have said?'

In other words, the educational value of improvised drama is inseparable from its 'togetherness', from the fun of having a go together, of exploring ideas together, of listening to each other, of adding to each other's ideas, of trying things out, of taking a possibly very ordinary or very dull 'starting point' and building on it. It is thus unlike something we do alone, and by its very nature and purpose cannot be done alone. Improvisation is not merely make-believe. It is not a story, a narrative. It is a make-believe story made up and acted out together. It is people interacting in a make-believe context. In this sense, it is social life, people coming together, but removed from the pressures and responsibilities (and limitations) of the real world.

Since the togetherness is 'what it's all about', improvised drama is (like most things) difficult to teach, for one is not simply teaching the subject-matter but, essentially, the way people can work together to explore the subject-matter. So a teacher knows he or she is beginning to get somewhere when the class appear to enjoy coming together, to appreciate each other's ideas, to pardon each other's lapses into embarrassing megalomania, or what have you, and, in a word, to *trust* one another. This is difficult to achieve, but no matter how elusive such trust may be, without a fair amount of it, improvised dramatic sessions will be of little educational value.

4 *What is the place of improvised drama in the curriculum?*
If we limit ourselves to the type of curriculum-organisation we are likely to meet in most secondary schools, we could argue that improvised drama might reasonably be employed within all those subjects that are concerned with the way people behave towards each other, with human motivation. The list would include: history; religious instruction; English language and literature. It would also include a number of subjects that appear on some school time-tables but by no means on all of them: psychology; sociology; business management; law; moral education; drama; film; media studies; sex education; current affairs; theatre arts. In all of these subjects, the focus at some time or other is drama — people interacting, and in all of them dramatic improvisations could be valuable ways of exploring, elaborating and illustrating the material in hand. And I hope that people teaching any of these subjects will find some parts of this book helpful in suggesting ways of approaching improvisation within their particular fields.

If all of these subjects can be seen as offering legitimate opportunities for improvisation, who has the best opportunity? Where might a headmaster, for instance, most expect to find a continuing and developing programme of improvisation? The answer is undramatic: wherever there are sustained opportunities to take a variety of starting points and to explore them in a variety of ways, including the use of improvisation. Within the time-table as it tends to be at present, the prize-winning candidate is probably *English*, in that the English Department has responsibility for the development of the whole range of language skills, and a fair amount of *lesson-time* in which to pursue a range of subject-matter and a range of activities. A specialist *drama department*, all things being equal, is likely to be most conscientious about seeking to develop improvised drama, but it is worth noting (a) that improvisation is only one of many activities central to drama, and (b) that most classes will have so few lessons with the drama specialist, that there will simply not be time (apart from exceptional cases) for the teacher to develop a relationship with the class or to bring in a variety of starting points and material. For instance, in many secondary schools the specialist drama teacher sees his or her class, on average, once a week for less than an hour.

I think that the drama specialist has most to offer when given the chance to work, therefore, within another department, or as part of a team covering a range of subjects. This may be as an 'English' teacher with particular responsibility (or just enthusiasm!) for developing improvised drama, or it may be as a member of a team teaching, say, the humanities. In either event, there is a real chance to employ improvisation across a range of starting points, and with time for the work to be discussed and developed.

5 *Finally, what is the teacher's role?*
Fundamentally, of course, improvised drama requires the same skills and techniques as does any other subject. The teacher needs to be able to achieve good discipline, so that a class know what is expected of them and can feel that good work is being done; he or she needs personal confidence, so that there can be a good rapport with the class and people can get on with the work in a relaxed and purposeful fashion. Much of the time, the skills are no different from those required in extending students' ability or experience in 'creative writing' or in good discussion. Specifically, I would isolate the following aspects of the teacher's role:

Setting up the lesson
Teachers quite rightly spend a great deal of time (and sometimes of anxiety) in deciding upon a good stimulus for dramatic work. A number of practical points can be made about this:
(i) Whatever stimulus you use, it has to be so well presented that it would stimulate you yourself, if you were a student in the class. This is an obvious enough point, but one easily forgotten. If, for instance, the particular stimulus is a literary excerpt which you read to the class, practise it beforehand, read it dramatically (not melodramatically) and clarify any names, words, phrases, or other details, as and when you think it is appropriate. If it is a story about a pirate, say so. If it is an ironic story, in some way indicate this. Follow the good precept of the cinema, the television and the bookshop. Don't just deliver the goods, advertise them, sell them well, urge the purchaser to purchase, make him eager to buy.

If the stimulus is an anecdote of some kind, perhaps a personal experience of your own, which you tell the class, the same principle applies. Make it a pleasure to listen to. Develop your own skill as a talker and teller.
(ii) A good stimulus, in general, is one that sets us off discussing and

story-telling; it reminds us of other experiences, and leaves us keen to argue the issues it raises. The teacher should, in a sense, do his or her homework beforehand to ensure that he can throw into the melting-pot *other stimuli* — these may be personal reminiscences, anecdotes, contentious points, questions, other literary excerpts and so on. It is not a matter of changing the stimulus, so much as reinforcing it.

(iii) In effect, the recurring questions in any improvisation-session are simple and few:
> what has happened here?
> why?
> has anything like this ever happened to us?
> what do we think about it?
> what might happen next?
> what would you do IF this happened to you?

It must be stressed that most classes will need a great deal of practice and opportunity before they can engage in good, open-ended discussion, exploring ideas together, listening to each other. But this is precisely what the teacher is there for — to create such opportunity. Again, I think it is important that the teacher should himself be able to answer, however tentatively, all the questions he raises. I am not encouraging here a situation in which the teacher answers his own questions and nobody else does. Simply, that the teacher in this way can genuinely help the class towards opening up their thinking, increasing their own contributions to the lesson, for in this way he is able to give them new models of the sort of activity he is asking them to pursue. Through his anecdotes, his questions, his reservations, and so on, they see some of the scope for their own involvement.

(iv) Do not give up too soon! I think we often abandon ship not because we lack faith in the material, but because we wrongly conclude a lack of interest from the whole class. We are perhaps too sensitive to their apparent preferences. Likewise, any response that is genuine, that actually says something about the material itself, is a valid starting point for talk: how do others feel? what would you say if....? Stanislavsky repeatedly makes the point that actors cannot play Shakespeare meaningfully, unless they can relate Shakespeare's characters to their own personal experience. The same is true of all the material we encourage a class to discuss and improvise. But it does not mean that we can only bring into such sessions material culled from the child's backyard, and more than that we whould only ask actors to play themselves. The fun, and the education, lie in building bridges where, often, none appears to exist. And this is where the teacher's role is paramount.

Organisation
The classic pattern of sessions in improvisation, will involve an alternation

between class work and group work, and may follow some such pattern as this:
- teacher sets up an initial stimulus with whole class;
- this is followed by some kind of class discussion;
- the class break into groups to work out an improvisation, spending some of the time talking about it, and some time actually doing it;
- while this is happening, the teacher goes round to each group, and joins in the discussions, perhaps, or even in the improvisation itself;
- the groups show their work to each other;
- the work is discussed, and some kind of follow-up is perhaps suggested, which may relate it to other work — as when the class use the dramatisation as a basis for creative writing.

It's easy enough to describe this kind of organisation. Teachers often find it falls down somewhere in the middle. In particular, they find it difficult to *be helpful* when they go round to each group. If a group have expired for lack of ideas or enthusiasm, while the next group are working with enough energy and interest to last them for the rest of the week, what does the teacher do?

In essence, I think that there are three different types of problem encountered by students when they are improvising, and the teacher's contribution to the solving of these problems is slightly different in each instance.

There is, *first*, the problem of *form*: the stimulus may be highly stimulating, but the improvisers are not able to translate it into a workable form. At times, this is because they are taking a stimulus which is already enveloped in form, but of a very different kind. For example, youngsters often seek to improvise a well-loved TV series, *Starsky and Hutch*, say, or a popular character from the movies, such as James Bond. But these are already 'formed' in the language of film, and it is difficult enough even to tell the story of a Bond movie, let alone to act it out as an improvisation. The movie-makers, after all, had the facilities not only of script and actors, but also of the elaborate technology of the cinematic cameras and of the various machines, rockets, and what you will, in front of which they set their cameras. One can fantasise one's private dramatisation of such things, in one's mind's eye, but to act it out together, meaningfully, is another matter entirely. It can be done, though, for all that, and this is where the teacher can help, for he can lead the group to re-think the material for the form in which they are now working. Indeed this is something which all improvisers have to do, even if the problem is not always as difficult: we re-think and extend the form. We ask questions such as:
- would the play work better with a commentator?
- can we focus on a particular moment or scene which particularly lends itself to verbal interaction?
- could we devise a framework for a sequence of scenes?

could we have a follow-up scene to show what was going on elsewhere at the same time? (— what Alfred Hitchcock calls a 'meanwhile back on the farm' scene)
could we have two scenes going on simultaneously?
could we have 'asides', or 'soliloquys', or could we use the 'voice over' to reveal the character's inner thoughts?
could we devise a 'fantasy' sequence?

In effect, one encourages the students to explore all the various conventions and techniques of the professional dramatic artist, and to find ways of utilising them within the framework of group improvisations.

The *second* problem, I would identify as a problem of *subject-matter*. If all drama is to do with people inter-acting, one could say that students can improvise any subject-matter which in any way is *relevant* to them, to their lives and experiences. And the teacher can help them to find this relevance in two ways. First, by getting them to ask and to talk about the questions I have already mentioned:
what is this about?
what would you do *if* this happened to you?
has anything *like* this ever happened to you?
what might happen next?
what might have happened before this?
what sort of people is this happening to?
can we introduce a new character?
can we change characters?

In effect, the teacher in such cases, is helping the group to go beyong their present thinking; perhaps he is literally taking the end of their dramatisation and inviting them to see it as a starting-point. The plane crash becomes the prelude to, say, a flash-back to the earlier lives of the travellers, or to an inquiry into what happened, and so on.

The teacher will also invite the group to look more closely at, and into, *the material itself*. Suppose, for example, the subject is historical. In the dramatic work, the class will on the one hand be asking how the material relates to themselves, what analogies they can draw with their own experience, and on the other hand they will be finding out more about the historical subject-matter. In effect, there is always this two-way process in all learning: what can I find out about the subject? and how can I relate it to myself? Hence the group improvising will sometimes be able to extend their work through research of various kinds, through finding out more about the actual subject. Thus a drama lesson on the theme of, say, *Billy the Kid*, would involve us in two marginally distinct types of improvisation:

(1)   dramas rooted in parallel or analagous experiences of our own — when we have been criminals, or hunted, or outlawed; and,
(2)   dramas rooted in a growing understanding of the actual evidence

related to Billy the Kid himself.

Obviously, all good work will in some way be a fusion of both, but it is worth spelling out that the work draws on these two rather different sources. One might say, that one of these sources is personal, is rooted in our own lives, and the other is external, is rooted in objective evidence of a great variety of kinds, such as works of history, of journalism, literature, and so on. And the teacher's opportunity is to work within *both* territories.

The *third* problem is one of *working together*. Most of the time, a class will work cheerfully in groups, and students enjoy the chance to share ideas, to talk things through. When a particular group finds this difficult, the teacher will of course employ the various techniques and ask the various questions outlined above. In addition, the teacher may also perhaps encourage members of the group to take roles outside the improvisation itself. One of them might be the director, for instance, and he or she might work out the overall shape of the scene together with the cues for different entrances and exits. A talent to direct, rather in the tradition of the film director as 'auteur', is an instinctive and as important as the talent to act.

A futher technique is for the teacher to participate in the improvisation itself, taking a part and gently leading others towards taking parts or extending them. This is a method perhaps chiefly associated with Dorothy Heathcote, and the various televised examples of her work have brilliantly demonstrated her work. Like all methods of teaching, it has its attendant dangers, including that of dominating the students' initiative and ideas. Everything depends on the confidence and flair of a particular teacher, and some teachers find it very difficult to step into a dramatic session in this particular way. I think it is valuable if they have a go at doing so at some time or other. Similarly, I suspect that it is a mistake to do so too often.

A further problem pertains to working together with the limited facilities available. While, obviously, a well equipped studio is the ideal setting, I would argue that much can be done even within the most cramped of classrooms. If the noise causes alarm in adjacent rooms, then the teacher can perhaps reduce the time spent on group work until the class have acquired the right (and elusive!) combination of effort and economy – but it is far better to do what you can in the classroom than to do nothing at all. The lack of space for movement is equally prohibitive, but again, I suggest that the teacher and class must experiment, and see what can be done.

Setting up structured improvisations
Some of the material in this book is designed for *free improvisation*: after discussion, the groups go away and work from the generalised starting-

point, developing it as they choose. Other material is *structured*: the starting-points are more specific, and a certain shape to the drama is built into the work from the start. How is such a session set up? There are several points:

(a)   It is set up with the whole class; (occasionally you may wish to set it up as group activity, but in general, and especially at the start of a course, I suggest you use it with the whole class working as a single unit).

(b)   Individual players are chosen for specific roles.

(c)   The class hear all the instructions for all the characters, unless of course, they are participants in the drama, as when the whole class constitute a jury or a court of inquiry.

(d)   The individual players do *not* hear the instructions for the other players. They wait outside the room while these are given.

(e)   The improvisation takes place before the whole class.

(f)   In the discussion afterwards, the players reveal to each other anything in their characters or motivations that did not 'surface' in the improvisation itself.

(N B The structured improvisations in this book can be adapted to the needs of a particular class. For example, in most cases women's parts can easily be rewritten as men's, and so on.)

Follow-up work
This might include:
 using parts of the improvisation as starting points for further improvisation;
 using ideas as a basis for varying kinds of written work;
 bringing in new material (from literature, history, etc,) to illustrate the same theme;
 devising one's own structured improvisations;
 tape-recordings; photo-plays; filmed sequences.

Evaluation
The evaluation of our work reflects our aims and also determines our progress and development. These are some of the questions worth asking and exploring:

(a)   Are we using a developing range of starting points? Is the class able to respond to different types of topic and theme, different types of stimulus (literary excerpts, news stories, anecdotes, historical problems, for instance) and also to stimuli of differing complexity?

(b)   Through their dramatic work, are they extending their awareness? are they looking at something of the complexity of people and of relationships? are they 'seeing' more than they appear to start off by seeing?

(c)   Is the class starting to find its own stimuli? Are they bringing along

ideas from their own experience — from life and from art? Are they starting to devise their own structured improvisations?
(d) Are they internalising the techniques of discussion? are they beginning to listen to each other? to take up and develop each other's contributions?
(e) Are they able to work as a whole class, sustaining and extending ideas together?
(f) Are they able to work as groups? The best grouping is self-chosen: they group for a specific purpose and do so on a basis of shared preferences. Sometimes a student is left out, sometimes of his or her own volition. Is the class able to assimilate such a student into one of the groups?
(g) Are individuals taking part in a wide range of capacities? Are they for instance, joining in class discussion; telling anecdotes; taking minor roles in improvisations; taking major roles; willing to work with different groups?
All these are yardsticks by which we can judge progress. They can only be attained in part, and can only be attained at all if given the opportunities and if given varied opportunities.

The material in this book is presented under two broad headings — for 'younger' and for 'older' students. There is neither magic nor science in this classification, and I hope that teachers will dip into different parts of the book at different times and find useful ideas, useful starting points for their work. Of course an idea that really works will lead on to a variety of other ideas, other material.

In conclusion
I began by indicating that drama is a basic form of expression, of the 'making of meaning', and that it is related intrinsically to a small number of other basic forms. It is this relationship which outlines for us the teacher's role in improvised drama. Just as the same experience can provide the raw material for drama, lyric, narrative and symposium, so in a session of improvised drama the teacher is inviting the class not only to improvise, but also to discuss and evaluate (the symposium), to reminisce and anecdotalise (the narrative), and to explore their personal feelings (the lyric). In this way, all work in improvised drama is an important humanising force, leading us towards a greater awareness of the complexity of human behaviour and motivation, of what people do and why they do it.

1 Cheating

Cheats are universally unpopular. But it's not always easy to be sure that somebody suspected of cheating is actually guilty. And even those found guilty can sometimes give very good reasons for what they've done. As an example, take the following news story from the USA.

Cheating allegations shake West Point military academy
West point, the 174-year-old United States military academy, has been rocked by a cheating scandal. 49 cadets are accused of violating West Point's honour code by collaborating on a take-home examination.

Another cadet who told an officer that the 49 'did no more than anybody else' in collaborating, has himself been charged with tolerating such cheating by not reporting it, and has been placed in solitary confinement while awaiting trial.

West Point's honour code is strictly enforced at all times, and it states that 'a cadet will not lie, steal or cheat, or tolerate those who do'.

One reason for the cheating is that cadets are expected to cover so much ground academically that it is almost impossible for them to keep up. The academy admits that for many it is simply a question of trying to get by from day to day.

For discussion
1 Is cheating a serious offence?
2 Have you ever been involved in a case such as this?
3 Why do people cheat? Is it ever justified? What do you think about the reason given in this story?
4 If you were the Principal or Commanding Officer at West Point, would you expel the students who cheat? How else might you deal with them?
5 Devise a situation in which somebody is suspected of cheating at an exam, and seeks to defend himself/herself. *Improvise* the story. Concentrate on *different scenes* in which the accused shows different aspects of his/her character, such as scenes in the classroom, in the playground, at home, etc.

The Queen of Spades

People who cheat at cards have always been popular characters in films and fiction, if not in real life. In Alexander Pushkin's short story *The Queen of Spades* a young engineer, Hermann, desperately needs to win a large sum of money, and he hears of an aged Countess who (allegedly) knows how to guess three cards in succession with infallible accuracy. But she has never revealed her secret to any one. He finds out where the Countess lives, and hides himself away in her room:

> The maids took off her cap trimmed with roses. They removed the powdered wig from her grey, closely cropped head. Pins fell about her in showers. The silver-embroidered yellow dress fell at her swollen feet. Hermann witnessed the hideous mysteries of her toilet. At last the Countess put on a bed-jacket and a nightcap, sat down by the window in a big arm-chair, and dismissed her maids. They took away the candles. The Countess sat there, her face quite yellow, her flabby lips moving, her body rocking to and fro. Her dim eyes showed a complete absence of thought; looking at her one might have imagined that the horrible old woman was moving not of her own will, but under the influence of some hidden galvanic power.
> Suddenly an extraordinary change came over that dead face. Her lips ceased moving, her eyes brightened. A stranger was standing before her.
> 'Don't be alarmed, for Heaven's sake. Don't be alarmed!' he said, in a low and clear voice. 'I don't mean to do you any harm. I have come to beg a favour of you.'
> The old woman stared at him in silence, looking as though she had not heard him. Hermann thought she was deaf, and bending right over her ear, repeated what he had just said. The old woman said nothing.
> 'You can bring about my happiness,' Herman went on, 'and it will cost you nothing. I know you can guess three cards in succession. . .'
> He stopped. The Countess seemed to have grasped what was required of her and was trying to frame her answer.
> 'It was a joke,' she said at last. 'I swear it was a joke!'
> 'It's no joking matter,' said Hermann angrily. 'I swear to you. Your secret will not be wasted on me. . . Well?'
> He paused, waiting for her answer with trepidation. The Countess was silent.
> 'I implore you by all that is holy in life. Tell me your secret. What does it matter to you? Perhaps the price of it was some terrible sin, the loss of eternal bliss, a compact with the devil. . .'
> The old woman did not answer a word. Hermann got up.

The Queen of Spades

'Old witch!' he said, clenching his teeth. 'I'll make you speak then...'
With these words he took a pistol out of his pocket.
'I ask you for the last time — will you name me your three cards? Yes or no?'
The Countess made no answer. Hermann saw that she was dead.

From *The Queen of Spades* by Alexander Pushkin, Dent, Everyman's Library, 1933

For discussion
1 What might happen next?
2 The Countess says at one point that 'it was a joke'. How might the story be affected if it actually *was* a joke?
3 In effect, Hermann is trying to get a secret and successful way of cheating at cards. Can you think of any real-life situation in which such a secret might actually exist and be used? Devise and improvise it.
4 In what ways might Hermann obtain the secret even after the death of the Countess?
5 How do you think the Countess herself obtained the secret? Devise and improvise the scene.

* * *

Structured improvisation
This improvisation involves *the whole class* and *two individual members* of the class.

The setting is an *inquiry by the class* into allegations of cheating at an exam.

The situation (to be given to the whole class) is as follows:

The class have recently taken an important end-of-year examination to determine who will qualify to join a top band 'GCE' class next year. Competition is very high among the various members of this and other classes.

The examination *in History* is slightly different from that in the other subjects, for the students write it in their own time, and not in the examination room. They are given the set of essay titles one month before the examination, and they choose one and write a two-thousand-word essay in their own time. *The rules* are that students must work on the essay entirely on their own, and that they must on no account quote from or copy from books unless they clearly show what they are doing, and acknowledge their sources.

When the history exam results come out, two students share the top marks and the first position — Jack and Kate. But a few days after this announcement, the History Master says that he is cancelling their marks because he has discovered (a) that their two essays are remarkably similar, and one appears to have copied extensively from the other and (b) that both essays contain an entire paragraph which he now realises has been copied from the work of a famous historian (from C V Wedgwood's account of the trial of Charles I). This is extremely serious, because it means that Jack and Kate will probably be excluded altogether from the GCE class next year.

They are both considered good students, and no such charge has ever been made against them in the past. They insist that they are entirely innocent of both charges, that they have never copied from each other and never copied from a book. They demand a hearing, and the History Master agrees that the entire class should hold an inquiry at which they decide what should be done.

At the hearing everyone will be encouraged to ask questions to the two accused. After this, and after Kate and Jack may have made any further statements that they wish to offer, the class will vote by show of hand whether they believe the History Master should go ahead with the cancellation of their marks.

Individual instructions for KATE *and* JACK *together:* you are entirely innocent. You cannot imagine how this whole business has blown up. You have never copied from each other, and never copied from a book. You are extremely keen to do the GCE course next year. You are convinced that the class will support you, and will not allow you to be punished for something of which you are entirely innocent. Also, you hardly ever talk, or have talked, to each other.

For KATE *alone:* you are usually a hard-working, honest person. But you somehow forgot about writing the history essay until it was too late to do either the reading or the writing. Rather than fail the exam or get a low mark, you looked around for a good way of cheating, and seized the opportunity to remove Jack's essay from his satchel (unnoticed) one day when he was having lunch. You know Jack is clever, and writes good history essays. You were shrewd enough, of course, to adapt the essay, so that it was not obviously cribbed and copied. But it is possible that some paragraphs you copied more or less as they stood. You are now amazed and furious at subsequent developments. Jack of course knows nothing of what you have done, and you are determined that nobody else will. You will go to the grave, if needs be, protesting your innocence. If needs be, you will acuse Jack of copying from you.

For JACK *alone:* this is the most unpleasant thing that has ever happened to you. When your parents heard about it, they would not believe that

Cheating

you could ever be charged with such a thing, let alone that you could ever be guilty of it. And you have certainly, on no occasion, ever talked about your essays with Kate or shared ideas with her. Your father has made two suggestions: as regards the similarity between your essays and hers, he things it possible that she 'borrowed' your essay from your satchel, for you often brought it along to school while you were writing it. And as regards the business of certain passages being the same as those from a book, your father says this easily happens when a student *makes notes* on a book while he is reading it, and then uses the notes to write the essay. Sometimes the student unintentionally turns the notes back into their original form when he prepares the final essay. Your father says this is a common thing in colleges and universities, and although students are not allowed to do it intentionally, the authorities are prepared to turn a blind eye when it happens accidentially, as in your case. You are sure that this is what has happened here: you took notes from the C V Wedgwood book while you were reading, and then copied them up (innocently) for the essay. If needs be, you will make both these points at the Inquiry.

N B At the end of the Inquiry, the class should vote on the questions (1) Did Kate and Jack conspire together to cheat? If not, (2) Did Kate cheat alone? or (3) Did Jack cheat alone?

2 Friendship

(see also section 21 for the 'older' group)

First, a story about somebody who wanted to be a friend, but nobody wanted him, because he was always trying to beg or borrow what didn't belong to him. . . .

Sam, the Scrounger

I never have liked old Samuel, he's always scrounging things. Like one day he leans over to me in the Maths lesson and whispers loud enough for all the school to hear, 'Eh Kevin, lend me your bike tonight will yer?' I pretends I can't hear him so he calls out again to me, even louder than last time, 'Eh Kevin, lend me your bike tonight will yer?' I give him a dirty look but that don't mean anything to old Samuel. He just grins back at me and says, 'You're a pal you are, Kevin. You're a real pal.' But I wasn't going to lend him my bike.
Then he comes running up to me when I'm going out of school, but still I wouldn't lend it him.
'Well, what's the matter with yer, then?' says Sam. 'I thought you was my mate.'
'Then you thought wrong,' I says.
'Nah there's no cause to be unsociable,' says Sam. 'Don't we always share our fags then, like a pair of old pals?'
'No!' I says. '*You* share *mine*.'
'Nah don't be like that. I gotta go up the Common with old Burkey and the boys, aint I? Can't go up there without a bike, now can I?'
'Too bad. Be needing it myself tonight. See yer, Sam.'
'What yer need it for then?'
'I'm going up the Common myself, aint I, with old Hector.'
'Hector Turnpenny? That weed!'
'Yeah, that weed! He's my best friend, aint he.'
'Come on Kevin. Be a pal. Lend me your bike!'
'You're a scrounger you are, always lending things off people, and they don't get them back very often neither.'
'You watch what you're saying, young Kevin!'
'Scounger! Sam the scrounger!'

Half an hour later I was doing some shopping for my mum when suddenly this bloke bumps his bike into mine, and he roars out laughing,

Sam, the Scrounger

and it's Samuel again.

'Watcha Kevin — I got the bike yer see. Off one of my mates.'

'Yer,' I said, not very friendly. 'Whose is it?'

'Old Tommy Tuffin's, aint it.'

'Old Tommy Tuffin's grandpa's, more like it.'

'Ha, ha. Very funny. It's good enough to get me up the Common, aint it.'

'Well let's hope there aint no breeze, for your sake, or it'll fall to bits, won't it.'

'Eh Kevin. Lend me a fag, before you go. Eh?'

Well I didn't lend him a fag, but later that evening I was up the Common with Hector Turnpenny when Hector suddenly remembered something.

'Heh. Did you hear about Sam Ferguson?'

'What about him?' I says.

'Well he got run over by a steamroller, didn't he.'

'You're joking,' I says. And I really thought he was.

'No, straight off,' says Hector. 'He borrowed some old bike, and it didn't have no brakes, and he went smash into a steamroller down the High Street.'

'What — Sam Ferguson?'

'Yeah. Sam Ferguson.'

'But is he dead then?'

'I reckon he could be now.'

'How d'you mean?'

'Well they took him in the hospital, didn't they.'

I felt really sick and awful, cause if I'd lent him my bike like he asked me to, then the accident wouldn't ever have happened. Cause my bike's a new one, and Tommy Tuffin's is so old no one should ever have tried to ride it, it aint safe. And then I thought how I'd always hated poor Sam, and how he'd never really done anything bad to me. He was always scrounging, that's true enough, but then we've all got our faults — like my mum is always saying.

My only hope was that old Sam wasn't quite dead yet. So Hector and me went down to his house but there was no one there. So we picked a lovely bunch of flowers from his front garden and took them up to the hospital. And I said to the nurse there, 'These are for Sam Ferguson. Is he dead yet?'

From 'Sam the Scrounger', in *Stories for Improvisation* by Peter Chilver, Batsford 1968

For discussion

1 Improvise the story so far, and add what might happen next.
2 Re-tell the story, with Sam as the narrator.

3 Has anything like this ever happened to you? Have you ever refused to help someone undeserving, and then regretted it? Can you dramatise the incident?
4 Do you ever see yourself as a scrounger? Devise an incident, real or imaginary, in which you desperately need to 'scrounge' off someone.

* * *

Alexander the Great

Another aspect of friendship is of course, trust. Friends are people who can have absolute trust or confidence in each other. The following story shows an extreme instance of such trustfulness. Alexander the Great was the victim of many unsuccessful murder attempts. In this story, probably a true one, he is sick, and attended by his doctor. But as the doctor gives him some medicine, Alexander receives warning that the medicine is probably poisoned.

> However it happened that none of his physicians would venture to give him any remedies, they thought his case so desperate, and were afraid that the Madedonians would suspect their intentions if the remedy should fail of its purpose. But Philip the Acarnanian, seeing how critical his case was, and relying on his well-known friendship for Alexander, resolved to try the last efforts of his art and to hazard his own reputation and life rather than suffer him to perish for want of physic. So he confidently administered a special potion to him. But at this very time Alexander received a message from one of his lieutenants, bidding him have care of Philip as one who was bribed by the Persian emperor Darius to kill him, with great sums of money and a promise of his daughter in marriage. When he had perused the message he put it under his pillow, and when Philip came in with the potion he took it from him with great assurance and cheerfulness, giving him meantime the message to read. And so it happened that as Alexander took the draught so Philip read the message. Philip asked Alexander to lay aside all fear, but the open and kindly looks of Alexander's face told him that he had the total confidence of his friend. Now the medicine worked so strongly that Alexander lost his speech, and falling into a swoon, had scarce any sense or pulse left. However in no time, by Philip's means, his health and strength returned, and he showed himself in public to the Macedonians, who were in continual fear and dejection until they saw him abroad again.
>
> From *Plutarch's Life of Alexander,* Dryden edition, translated by A H Clough, Dent, *Everyman's Library* 1910

For discussion

1. This is a specially dramatic example of a friend's trust in another friend. How do we know who to trust?
2. Why are some people more trusting than others? Why are some more trustworthy than others?
3. Has there ever been a similar instance in your own life when you have trusted someone, a friend, despite every suggestion that you should not do so? Improvise the story.
4. Devise a scene in which you encourage someone to trust you.
5. Devise the same scene with two entirely different endings.

* * *

Z cars

In the play *Window Dressing*, written by Ronald Eyre for the television series 'Z Cars', two young men, working in a store, decide to play a joke on their employer. They break into the store at night and rearrange some of the goods. But the joke goes too far, and serious damage is caused. And the two friends, in effect, tell on each other. In the first extract, Inspector Watt is talking to Greenhalgh:

GREENHALGH	I was on my way home.
WATT	Where do you live?
GREENHALGH	New Street.
WATT	Do they know you're out?
GREENHALGH	I expect so.
WATT	Why are you so late going home?
GREENHALGH	Been out.
WATT	Where've you been?
GREENHALGH	Look. Do I have to explain everything? I was only
WATT	passing the door.
GREENHALGH	Were you loitering? Where've you been? Had a few drinks.
WATT	You're under age, aren't you?
GREENHALGH	You asked me where I'd been. I've had a few drinks.
WATT	By yourself?
GREENHALGH	Some of the time.
WATT	Who were you with the rest of it?
GREENHALGH	Friends.
WATT	Who?
GREENHALGH	A friend.
WATT	What's his name?
GREENHALGH	Do I have to give names?

WATT	Nobody's accusing you of anything, lad. I'm asking questions. If you know the answers, you'd better tell me who you were with.
GREENHALGH	Gordon Plimmer.
WATT	Gordon Plimmer. Well that's all I asked you. We want you to help us, that's all. Nobody's forcing you.

Later, the Inspector calls on Plimmer:

WATT	Now, Terry Greenhalgh. He's a friend of yours. (There is no reply) And you were with him last night?
PLIMMER	No.
WATT	He says you were.
PLIMMER	He would. He's barmy.
WATT	(Opens his notebook.) Right. Now. About Mercer's. Tell me if I'm wrong. Broke in. Smashed crockery, broke kitchen utensils, left tap running in cloakroom, pounds worth of damage by water, front door left open. Theft of goods. (Plimmer is amazed) Anything to add before I take you off?
PLIMMER	We didn't do any of that.
WATT	I thought you weren't there.
PLIMMER	It's not us.
WATT	Want to come and have a look?
PLIMMER	You're after somebody else.
WATT	Why didn't you tell me then? You could have saved me a lot of time.
PLIMMER	I didn't know what you wanted.
WATT	But you'd got something to hide, hadn't you? Eh?
PLIMMER	You and Terry Greenhalgh.
WATT	We didn't do all that.
PLIMMER	What did you do then?
WATT	We had, more like, a laugh.

From Ronald Eyre, *Window Dressing*, Longman's Imprint Books 1968

For discussion

1 The stories we tell usually change as we tell them to different people. Devise and improvise situations in which the two boys tell what happened to friends, their family, the police, the magistrate.
2 Devise and improvise the scene where the boys decide to break into the store.

Friendship

3 Devise the scene where they meet up again at the police station.
4 In this play, a more or less innocuous joke turns nasty. How did this perhaps happen? And –
5 Has such a thing ever happened to you, or to anybody you know? (This might not be anything so dramatic as a criminal offence.)

* * *

Structured improvisation

Two characters, schoolboys, TOM and BILL.

Instructions for BOTH CHARACTERS: Tom and Bill are firm friends, with a shared enthusasm for football, which they enjoy watching and playing. They both play for the School first eleven football team, and Tom became the captain of the team a few weeks ago. They are very good players, and Bill has ambitions to take up professional football when he leaves school. Tom has no such ambition, but hopes eventually to train as a solicitor.

Instructions for TOM: (alone) The master who runs the football team has suggested to you that Bill is not really up to standard for the school first eleven, and advises dropping him in favour of someone else. Because Tom is such a good friend you are very reluctant to do this, and have said so to the master. But he has insisted that Bill must go. Now it just so happens that a new teacher has come to the school, who is keen to introduce rugby and is busily recruiting new players. You have used your influence to recommend Bill, and you intend to persuade Bill to drop soccer and take up rugby, with a view to his becoming captain of the rugby team. You know that it will be difficult to get Bill to do this, since he thinks he's very good at soccer. The task will require great skill.

Instructions for BILL: at the last match, your father brought along a representative from a professional team. He was so impressed by you, that he is going to bring someone else to the next match, and it is possible that this will lead to your being invited to train professionally. Nobody else knows about this, but you think you must now tell Tom.

The two meet at school, during the lunch-hour.

3 Running Away

Schoolboy missing from home for a fortnight

Local schoolboy Henry Brown has been missing from his home in Ryeslip Avenue for the past two weeks.

The 15-year old youth had been ordered by his parents to stay at home for being disobedient. But during the evening he slipped out without telling them and when he hadn't returned the following morning, Mr and Mrs Brown told the police.

Although it is now two weeks since Henry ran away, his mother is sure he is safe and well. She commented, 'Several people have told me that they have seen Henry in the district, so at least I know nothing has happened to him. I think it is a matter of time before he returns home.'

Five feet, four inches tall, Henry left home wearing a mauve shirt, blue pullover, green trousers and a three-quarter-length fur-trimmed car-coat.

His mother doesn't think he had very much money when he left but she suspects he is being looked after by some of his friends.

For discussion

1 From the news report, how much do we learn about Henry, his family, and why he left home?
2 Improvise the scene where the parents decide to phone the police. Perhaps add the sequence where the police come to interview the parents.
3 Improvise other scenes, including (a) where Henry is disobedient and ordered to stay home, and (b) where Henry eventually returns (if you think he ever does!)
4 The film director Alfred Hitchcock has given the term 'meanwhile back on the farm scenes' to describe sequences where we are shown what is happening simultaneously to a sequence we have just seen. Devise a 'meanwhile back on the farm' scene showing Henry's whereabouts while his parents are contacting the police.
5 How do you think Alfred Hitchcock might dramatise (and film) this particular story?
6 Can you devise different stories (based on the same news report)

in which the *responsibility* for Henry's running away falls on *different* characters? Can you now devise one in which the responsibility falls evenly on all the characters?

* * *

Out of Bounds

Esmond Romilly was the son of a rich, aristocratic family, and a nephew of Winston Churchill. He was educated at a private 'prep' school and then at Wellington College — a 'public' school which he disliked very strongly. At the age of 15, while still at Wellington, he started publishing a magazine called 'Out of Bounds' in which he attacked public schools in particular and privilege in general. The magazine became notorious, though its sales were very modest. The *Daily Mail* published a leading article accusing Romilly of financial support from the Russian government. Romilly decided to devote himself full-time to his journalistic ambitions, and ran away. He published the magazine from various 'hideouts' in London, and later fought in the Spanish Civil War and reported on the War for the British press. On the outbreak of the Second World War he joined the Air Force and was killed in action.

He wrote his memoirs shortly after running away from school:

I was unable to enjoy the last few days at Wellington. I was far too anxious. Actually I had not settled on any definite plan. I told several friends I was leaving, and they thought I was wise in doing so, especially in view of the magazine which now obviously could not be produced at Wellington. Originally I had intended to leave on Saturday; then I altered the day to Thursday, and in the end I left at six o'clock on Friday morning. I realized that running away was going to be fairly difficult if I did not want to be hauled back early in the procedure. There was the difficulty of going down to the station with a heavy suitcase as well as the problem to face of ensuring myself sufficient start to avoid being stopped at Waterloo. . . . . It may seem strange that I wondered whether I ought to inform the Headmaster that I was leaving. I should have liked to have been able to explain to him my reasons, and also it would have been an act of courtesy after the remarkably kind way in which he had behaved towards me. It was however quite ridiculous to think of it. It would have been rather extraordinary for a boy to inform his Headmaster that he intended running away from school the next day. I had learned too that both Mr Malim and my father were in close and intimate contact with the Special Branch of the police. I knew nothing of the extent of their powers, or how far they would be prepared to use them, but I decided that a ride in a Black

Maria was to be avoided. . . . .
The next morning I bought three newspapers. To my great surprise all of them gave prominence to my exploit. This is what I saw:

> Mr Churchill's Nephew Vanishes
> Colonel's son runs away from School
> 'Under Influence of Communists' says Mother
> Secret Dash Out of College

From *Out of Bounds* by Esmond Romilly, Hamish Hamilton 1935

For discussion

1 Improvise the scene which might have taken place if Romilly *had* gone to the Headmaster and explained why he was leaving.
2 Improvise the scene where Romilly's mother meets the press.
3 What are the various reasons that prompt people to run away? In general, when is it right to run away? and when is it wrong?
4 Have you ever run away? Or wanted to run away?
5 Improvise different scenes in which different people seek to dissuade Romilly from running away — friends, teachers, relatives, strangers. Improvise scenes where people try to persuade him to *return*.
6 Improvise a press conference, at which Esmond faces the whole class (playing news reporters) and answers such questions as they think appropriate for explaining the runaway.

Perhaps stage other press conferences at which the central figure might be (a) the Headmaster or (b) the Mother.

* * *

News story (1)

Boy booted out of games by shame

Roger, aged 13, played truant every time his class had a sports day. He was scared of being punished by his teacher at a large comprehensive school because he had no football boots.

A school care worker with the Inner London Education Authority announced today that many children are staying away from school when PE or games are on the time-table rather than risk punishment or humiliation because they cannot afford the proper kit.

News story (2)

A chimney tomb for runaway

A frightened youth on the run from police thought he had found sanctuary — hidden up the chimney of a derelict shop.

But Brian Smith's hideout proved to be his grave. Builders found his skeleton trapped where he died in the sooty brickwork.

Murder Squad detectives yesterday identified 18-year-old Brian's skeleton from dentist's records. And they revealed how he had fled from a remand home sentence, only to find a far more terrible prison.

For discussion

1 Would you judge anyone to be responsible for the things that happen in these two news stories?
2 Improvise the first story. Build up a series of scenes to portray the character of Roger and the people around him.
   Include, perhaps, scenes at home, in the playground, in the classroom.
3 In what ways does the story change as Roger's character changes? (for example, suppose Roger is a fluent liar. . . .)
4 Brian, in the second story, takes an extreme step to save himself from the remand home. What kind of person is Brian likely to have been? Build up a character-sketch of him, of his background, family, schooling, etc. Invent possible incidents from his life. Improvise some of them.

* * *

Structured improvisation

Three characters: Mrs Edwards, and her two children, Jim aged 13, Sue aged 14.

Instructions for ALL THREE CHARACTERS: you are a reasonably happy, contented family. Father works on the railway, mother in an office. Sue is doing excellently at school. Jim is at the same school, not doing quite so well, but he is not an especially 'bad' pupil. There have been some complaints of rudeness and even of truancy, but nothing very serious. Father is strict, and is very much in charge of the family. (As an example, no money is ever given to either of the children except by Father.) *In this scene*, you are at home; it is early evening; Mrs Edwards is preparing supper. Jim comes home late, just as the scene begins, and Sue comes home a few minutes later, also late — but Mrs Edwards knows that she has been studying in the school library. Tonight, Mr Edwards will not be home for another couple of hours because he is on a late shift. The setting is the kitchen and sitting-room.

Individual instructions for MRS EDWARDS: you are worried today. Half an hour ago you were tidying the house, and in Jim's bedroom you found a letter he was writing to a friend. Jim doesn't know it, but you always read any letters that you find. This one revealed that he is in trouble at school, for being rude to the Deputy Head and also for truancy, and that he has decided to run away from home and join the Merchant Navy. He is quite big for his age, and he is convinced, apparently, that he will be able to masquerade as an older boy. And the friend, who is in the Navy already, will be able to help him. The letter shows that he plans to run away as soon as possible. You are not sure what to do next. You have put the letter back where you found it, and will of course tell your husband as soon as he gets home. But in the meantime, you plan to make sure (a) that Jim does not know you've seen the letter, and (b) that he doesn't get out of the house. You will have to find various jobs for him to do. But you are not a very strict parent, and you would much prefer not to have to deal with this at all. It might be possible to enlist Sue on your side: she is such a sensible girl. But you're not sure yet. . . .

Individual instructions for SUE: everyone thinks of you as a hard-working good girl, and you're very happy that they should carry on thinking this. But last week you met a pop star who was appearing at a local club (he is quite famous, and very rich and fascinating). He came to the school, in fact, to give a talk for a school music club, and you chatted with him afterwards and he offered to drive you home. His name is Gerry Robbins. He has waited for you every day after school since that first meeting, and today he suggested that you elope with him to London. You're keen to do so. He said it would be dangerous (illegal, in fact) to take you himself, in his car, and that the safe thing would be for you to run away on your own, take the train to London, and join him there. He offered you money, which you proudly refused to accept. But now you realise that you have no ready cash in the house. So you will have to borrow from your mother, or even from your brother (if he has any). But it is important that no one should suspect your motives, so you will have to invent a plausible reason for wanting the money so quickly (before father gets home, in fact, for he would never allow you out at the end of the evening.)

Individual instrucitons for JIM: a dramatic day. You've been accused of truancy, yet again — but all you ever do, in fact, is take the afternoon off when you're supposed to be at 'games' — which you hate. You have several times been up before the Deputy Head on account of this. This time, the Deputy Head says he will write to your father complaining of your behaviour and attendance. You've also been in trouble because of failure to do homework. This might not matter so much if you had not today become involved in 'the school play'. You are now an enthusiastic member of the school's production of *Oliver Twist* in which you are playing the Artful Dodger. You fear that the Deputy Head might decide to withdraw you from the cast, because of your various "misdeeds". The special attraction is that the cast have been invited to tour West Germany with the production at some future date. But you will need £20.00 for this, to cover plane fare and lodging. (The Education Authority pays the rest of the bill.) So you will try to win over your mother this evening, with a view to getting her on your side before you tackle your father.

You will also try to keep up with your various homework assignments, and in particular will want to finish off the imaginary letter you are writing for the English teacher, under the heading, 'Running Away'.

The scene begins with your coming home late — you have been at the very first rehearsal for *Oliver Twist*, which you attended just on the off-chance that you might like to have a small part, and were amazed (and delighted) to get a leading role, plus the chance of a continental tour.

Incidentally, on your way home, you were amazed to see your sister Sue in a car driven — you think — by a famous pop star, Gerry Robbins. He came to the school last week to give a talk for the music club, and you guess that Sue must have met up with him then. . . .

4 Espionage

There have always been spies. Alexander the Great, for instance, was constantly trying to separate them from his friends and advisers. And in our own time spies such as Lonsdale, Philby and Burgess have become (however briefly) household names. Equally famous are some of the great spies of fiction, such as James Bond.

What makes a good spy?

The CIA (Central Intelligence Agency) is an American organisation, financed by the Federal Government. Its function is (a) to engage in intelligence operations against countries or peoples who are considered hostile to the USA, and (b) to infiltrate the activities of enemy agents *within* the USA.

A former director of the CIA, Allen Dulles, was asked what were the qualities of a good intelligence officer. He listed the following:

Be perceptive about people
Be able to work well with others under difficult conditions
Learn to discern between fact and fiction
Be able to distinguish between essentials and non-essentials
Possess inquisitiveness
Have a large amount of ingenuity
Pay appropriate attention to detail
Be able to express ideas clearly, briefly, and very important, interestingly
Learn when to keep your mouth shut

Mr Dulles also suggested:

A good intelligence officer must have an understanding for other points of view, other ways of thinking and behaving, even if they are quite foreign to his own. Rigidity and close-mindeness are qualities that do not spell a good future in intelligence.
An intelligence officer must not be overambitious or anxious for personal reward in the form of fame or fortune. These he is not likely

to get in intelligence work.

> From *The Craft of Intelligence,* by Allen Dulles, Weidenfeld and Nicholson, London 1963

For discussion
1. Which of these qualities would you consider most important in espionage?
2. What other qualities might be important?
3. How would you discover if somebody has these qualities before employing him as a spy?
4. Have you ever spied on anyone? What happened?
5. Have you ever tried to persuade somebody else to spy?
6. Improvise a situation in which you engage in espionage.

* * *

The Philby Affair

Kim Philby is an Englishman who rose to high office in the British Secret Service during and after the Second World War. It was later discovered that he was in fact spying for the Russians. But as the evidence against him was accumulating, he fled to Russia and has lived there ever since. While he was working with the British Secret Service, he was asked to handle The Volkov Case, in which a Russian diplomat in Istanbul secretly asked the British Government for asylum in Britain for himself and his wife. In return he offered the British the names of various Soviet agents working abroad, including the names of two Soviet agents working in the Foreign Office, one of whom was involved in counter-espionage. This, of course, was Philby himself. But the British, unknowingly, gave Philby the job of looking into the Volkov case and of advising them what to do. Philby went to Istanbul, pretended to conduct proper investigations, and when the time seemed ripe, told the Russians. As a consequence, Volkov mysteriously disappeared and Philby was able to return to London and offer various explanations of what had happened. He remained in the British Service for several more years without exciting suspicion.

This is how Philby describes the incident in his memoirs:

> I stared at the papers rather longer than necessary to compose my thoughts. I rejected the idea of suggesting caution in case Volkov's approach should prove to be a provocation. It would be useless in the short run, and might possibly compromise me at a later date. The only course was to put a bold face on it. I told the Chief that I thought

we were on to something of the greatest importance. I would like a little time to dig into the background and, in the light of any further information on the subject, to make appropriate recommendations for action. The Chief acquiesced, instructing me to report first thing next morning and, in the meanwhile, to keep the papers strictly to myself. I took the papers back to my office, telling my secretary that I was not to be disturbed, unless the Chief himself called. I very much wanted to be alone. My request for a little time to dig into the background had been eye-wash. . . . The case was of such delicacy that the Chief had insisted on my handling it myself. But once the decisions had been taken in London, all action would devolve on our people in Istanbul. . . . The more I thought, the more convinced I became that I should go to Istanbul myself, to implement the course of action that I was to recommend to the Chief. . . . That evening I worked late. The situation seemed to call for urgent action of an extra-curricular nature. Next morning I reported to the Chief that the case was of great potential importance and I recommended, rather diffidently, that somebody fully briefed should be sent out from London to take charge of the case on the spot. 'Just what I was thinking myself' replied the Chief. But having raised my hopes, he promptly dashed them. His intention was to send Brigadier Douglas Roberts straight out to Istanbul to take charge of the Volkov case.

Adapted from *My Silent War* by Kim Philby, MacGibbon and Kee 1968

For discussion
1 Why did Philby not tell the Russians to remove Volkov there and then?
2 How might Philby have persuaded his Chief to send him, and not Roberts, to Istanbul?
3 In persuading the Chief to change his mind, Philby would have to be careful to remain calm, and not to show too much concern. Can you think of any occasion when you have in any way been in a similar position?
4 The Chief was of course, deceived by Philby, so were many other officials in high positions in the British Government. Have you ever been seriously deceived by others? Have you ever yourself been the deceiver?
5 *Improvise* (a) the above scene from the Philby story, and (b) a possible sequel when Philby gets to Istanbul and perhaps meets Volkov. (NB Volkov would not have known Philby *by name* as a Russian agent.)
6 Improvise a parallel situation from your own experience, or from the experience of someone you know.

Informers

There are other kinds of spies, of course — including those who spy on industries, and also those who spy on gangs of criminals and who then relay their information to the police. Sometimes these informers are themselves criminals, and very often when they 'inform' on friends or rivals they secure a slightly more lenient sentence as a reward for their services. (Sometimes the reward is more substantial, for they may not be prosecuted at all.) What follows is a brief extract in which the writers look at the ways in which crime changes as more and more thefts and robberies become major operations involving the co-operation of whole teams of criminals, rather than individual acts performed by individual actors:

> He is vulnerable because of the relatively long time it takes to assemble a team and plan and co-ordinate a job. This second feature of the work has introduced a whole new element into police-criminal relations, since it makes it possible for detectives to discover crimes before they are committed and so either prevent them or arrange to catch the criminals red-handed. The police rely more and more on informers from within the underworld and on infiltration into the underworld by 'ghost squad' detectives. This means that the underworld is no longer a milieu of safety for the thief. His response has been to live as much as possible as an apparently ordinary citizen, often with a legitimate occupation as a front, and to communicate with his colleagues in roundabout and secretive ways.

From *Images of Deviance* edited by Stanley Cohen

For discussion
1. The criminal who informs on other criminals, performs a useful service to society. How do we ourselves feel about informers?
2. Have we ever informed on others? Or encouraged others to be informers? *Improvise* such a situation.
3. We can usually give very good reasons for everything we do.
   Devise and improvise a situation in which an informer so well justifies himself that he might even convince the person against whom he has informed.
4. Devise and improvise a situation, as above, (a) in a setting outside school and (b) inside school.

Espionage

Structured improvisation

There are four characters, two boys, two girls.

Instructions for ALL THE CHARACTERS: the four of you are close friends, and attend this school. You have from time to time over the last year or so, operated secretly as a gang of thieves — a kind of modern equivalent to Robin Hood, stealing from the rich to give to the poor. Your method is that one of you knocks at the front door of a rich-looking household, and asks for a non-existent person who (you pretend) you think lives there. While you are doing this, the other three go round the back of the house, and if you are satisfied that nobody else is at home, you discreetly enter the house, remove something small but valuable (preferably cash) and make your getaway. You always give the proceeds to someone in need, and always do this anonymously. A month ago, you stole from a lady down the road, and gave the proceeds to a poor widow, leaving the money in an envelope, again giving no indication of the names of the donors. But the widow told the local press, and the story has been published under the heading, 'Good Samaritan Stays Anonymous'. No connection has been made, though, between the gift and any thefts. TODAY all four of you meet up at Linda's house, to play what to do next.

Individual instructions for ANN: you became involved in the gang, because you like Jack, and because Linda is your best friend. But you find it very frightening and have decided that enough is enough. You decide to drop out of the gang, and intend to tell them so today at the meeting. You think your Mother suspects something too.

Individual instructions for TOM: unknown to the others, you have frequently stolen more than you have handed over, and so you have in fact been making a personal profit on the adventures. Last time you kept £30 in cash from the lady's handbag, which none of the others knew about. You are greedy for more, and so you plan to drop out of the gang and find someone else to work with — only one, so that you don't have to share the proceeds with others. But you have no intention of letting the rest of the gang know what's happening. So your story will be that you've got to do more homework in order to pass your exams, and that at any rate you are afraid of the police finding out what's been going on.

Individual instructions for LINDA: your Mother happens to be a friend of the last victim of the gang's thieving, and in this way you have learned that more money was in fact stolen than was ever handed over to the poor widow. You were so disgusted to hear this that you at once told your Mother *everything*. But she is so used to your talent for story-telling and exaggeration that she refused to believe you. In despair you told a boyfriend who works as a reporter on a local newspaper, and he suggested that you hold a meeting of the gang at your house, plan another robbery, and keep a small tape recorder carefully hidden at which you record everything that is said. You're not quite sure what he will do with the recording. Take it to the police, perhaps. So you will have to be careful what *you* say. . . .

Individual instructions for JACK: you very much enjoy the adventure of the various robberies, and of giving the money to those in need. You are very fond of Ann, and slightly suspicious of Tom. You even have an idea that he joins in the thefts too enthusiastically, and perhaps keeps back some of the proceeds for himself. But you have no evidence. Your latest plan is to rob a rich uncle of yours — with Linda acting as the decoy who knocks on the door. You are aware that stealling is immoral and illegal, but you feel that the good things you do with the stolen money cancel out the wrongs that you inflict.

The scene begins at Linda's home, as all four arrive and Linda makes tea for them.

5 The Big and the Small

'The Big versus the Small' is one of the classic themes of folklore and literature. So is the small man's desire to be big. . . . The hero of David Walker's novel is 14, and known as 'Wee Geordie':

Geordie

> There were some old magazines in the corner of the room. Geordie had read them all before, for he was a great reader, even if reading took time, because he was slow in his thoughts as well as in his growing. There were some adventure stories and some about love. He never bothered with the love ones. Love was daft. But he liked fine to read adventure.
> Here was page 46 and. . . . But Geordie stopped. He was seeing something he'd never noticed any of the other times. It stood up on the printed page and it smacked him in the eye. He looked away to go on reading the story, and looked back again. That was how it smacked him.
> It was an advertisement, tucked up there in the corner, an advert with two small pictures. Geordie read it through once. Then he read it again. This is what he read:
>> 'Are you undersized? Do people ignore you? No need for despair. Grow big the Samson way. Write for my only unique course in physical culture. You can be strong. You can be tall. Balanced development is my motto. World-wide testimonials. For proof of success see untouched photographs below.
>> 'Send ten shillings only for complete course in plain wrapper. Your problems will receive personal attention of the great Henry Samson, six foot four and the world's strongest man.
>> 'Write PO Box 689, Wandsworth, London, SW. Satisfaction guaranteed.'
> Geordie suddenly felt very tired. Perhaps it was just the great idea striking him. Yes, it must be that. He closed his eyes for a minute, lying quite slack, seeing wonderful pictures of him big and strong. Then he opened his eyes again to read the advert. The man was a wee stoopy thing BEFORE, but he had a chest like a barrel on him AFTER, and tall.

Ten bob was a big price. It was a huge price; and how would you know it wasn't just a have-on?... Generally Geordie took a long time to decide things; but not now. He'd made up his mind already what he had to do, and he knew that the Samson course, English or no, was a right good bargain. He was sure of it. What was ten bob if you could be as big as Henry Samson?.....

He put the address on the top and then he wrote:

> Dear Sir (Mister Henry Samson)
> Please send by return complete course to yours trooly in plain wrapper. I am fourteen past and wee for my age, so I need hight and strength. Her is ten shillings in a P.O.
> Hoping this finds you as it leaves me, in the pink.
> Geordie Mactaggart

Geordie wrote the envelope too. He put it all away for Monday morning when he'd go to the post office before school. Then he went down for his tea.

From *Geordie* by David Walker, Collins 1958

For discussion

1 What might happen next?
2 Is the course likely to be a success or a failure? What will its effect be, in either case, upon Geordie himself?
3 Improvise the story. Include sequences to show why Geordie cares so much about his appearance.
4 'Henry Samson' makes money, presumably, out of other people's feelings of inferiority. What other ways are there of making money out of such feelings? Incorporate one of them into a story and improvisation.
5 Is it silly to feel inferior about one's physical appearance?
6 What in general is our attitude towards our own inferiority? Are we in any way like Geordie — anxious to change, by miracle if need be, whatever makes us look small in the eyes of others?

* * *

The following is a news story about something very small that 'grew' into something very big:

Bus fare for white mouse

Local schoolgirl Linda Farrell was today charged an extra fare of sevenpence for the white mouse she was carrying in a small white box.

The incident occurred when Linda, travelling with her grandfather, was asked by the conductor to explain the squeaks coming from the box. When she told him it was her four-week-old pet mouse, the conductor checked the regulations and told her the mouse counted as livestock and livestock must be paid for.

Linda refused to pay the extra money, but after some delay, when the driver refused to take the bus any further until the fare was settled, Linda's grandfather paid the money for her.

Linda's parents say, 'We are disgusted with the whole thing, and intend to complain to the Bus Company.'

A few days later, the plot thickened:

Bus company consider bus fare for mouse

The NEB Bus Company said today that many complaints had been received about the extra fare paid for local schoolgirl Linda Farrell's white mouse-in-the-box.

Company officials will consider the case at their meeting tomorrow.

Controversy over the case became nation-wide after Linda (and her mouse) were interviewed on BBC TV Tuesday evening. Linda told how the conductor had read the regulations to her, but she said, they said nothing about mice of any colour.

The conductor was not available for comment.

And finally:

Mouse's bus fare refunded

NEB Bus Company officials, at their monthly meeting, today agreed to refund to Linda Farrell (and her grandfather) the sevenpence bus fare demanded for her white mouse.

An official spokesman said the conductor had acted properly and conscientiously in charging the fare, but that the Company did not classify a white mouse as livestock. 'It is too small', said the spokesman.

The Company have written to Linda offering her the refund, any time she calls in to the Company offices. But Linda's grandfather says that the money should be sent through the post. 'It will cost us more than that in bus fares to go down and collect the refund', he said.

For discussion

1. Improvise the scene on the bus.
2. Improvise the scenes (a) at home after Linda's return (b) at the TV interview (c) at the Bus Company meeting.
3. How many different ways can you find to *characterise* the leading

characters in the story? (For example, can Linda be protrayed as *very* shy?. . .)
4 How does the scene change as different 'minor' characters are introduced? — as for instance, when different passengers come onto the bus.
5 Could the story have 'grown bigger'? Could it, plausibly, have snowballed into a major incident? How could this have happened?
6 Have you ever been involved in a similar incident?
7 Take the principal characters in turn, and interview them.
8 In a case like this, is it possible to say that anyone is in the wrong?

* * *

Structured inprovisation

For TWO CHARACTERS: Joe, aged 13, Derek aged 12.
Instructions for JOE and DEREK: you are both at the same secondary school. Joe is a year ahead of Derek. You have seen each other, vaguely, but do not know each other to speak to. Derek is already well known in the school, for he is a champion boxer, and has just recently won a major prize at an inter-schools boxing competition. *The scene takes place* in the bicycle shed at school, very late in the afternoon, about an hour or so after the end of school.
Individual instructions for JOE: when you were at primary school you knew a boy named Georgie Smith, who was a year younger than you, and you used to bully him and frighten him to death. You are in general a very nice person, but you find Georgie an irritating and weak individual, and you cannot resist the temptation to upset him. In fact you loathe fighting, and would never fight anyone unless you absolutely had to. But you never fought Georgie — just scared him. In fact, you blackmailed him. You somehow led him to believe that he had broken your fountain pen, a present from your father, and you made him pay you the price of a new pen by weekly instalments. You came to the High School a year before he did, and you lost contact with him. But now he is in the year below you, and you have decided to sieze the chance to get more money from him. So you have ganged up on him with some of your friends, and scared the life out of him — again. And he has sworn to resume payments to you — 50 pence a week for the next six weeks, commencing today. You have arranged to meet him in the bicycle shed after school. He is late, but you are still waiting. In fact, you are desperate to see him and to take the money from him and indeed, to take more if you can manage it, for over the weekend you borrowed three pounds from your father without

telling him, and spent it, and you have no means of paying the money back to your father. As soon as your father finds out, you will be in serious trouble.

Georgie Smith has not yet appeared; but while you are waiting you see Derek come along. You've never spoken to him, but you know he's a champion boxer, and he seems a very pleasant person. You would like to get to know him. . . .

Individual instructions for DEREK: there is a boy called Georgie Smith in your class, and he often helps you out with homework – letting you copy his notes, and sums, and so on. You do not have a lot of time to do your homework because, of course, you are busy training for your boxing contests. You think you might one day be a professional boxer. Georgie has told you about a boy named Joe in the second year who bullies him and demands money from him, and has been doing so since they were at primary school together. It seems that Joe has invented some story about Georgie having broken his father's fountain pen (!) and has made Georgie pay for the pen in never-ending instalments. You know that Joe is waiting now for Georgie to come and hand over some more money (50 pence today) and you have told Georgie to go home and forget about it: you'll see this Derek yourself and deal with him. Not only that, but you'll get back from him the money that has already been paid over. You gather that Georgie has in fact paid at least four or five pounds over the last couple of years. You detest bullies, and are determined to protect Georgie. But you have to be careful. On no account are you to strike Joe, or to provoke a fight, for that would get you into trouble in school and might lead to your expulsion from the boxing contests. So you will have to use the power of persuasion, and of subtle threat. (Also, you have promised Georgie that the story will not leak out to anyone else, such as the teachers.)

The scene begins with Joe waiting near his bike, and Derek coming from a practice-session in the gymnasium.

6 Family Life

'One very hot day, ages ago, my younger brother suddenly asked my mother for a button-collar shirt. Point-blank — while she was doing the washing. He was a quiet boy, and for him to ask for something out of the blue like that was unusual to say the least. But he did — and unfortunately at that time my mother couldn't afford it. So she wiped her hands carefully, put her wedding ring back on, and said no. . . .'

This is how *Ray Jenkins* explains the source of his idea for his short play *Five Green Bottles*. Here is a short extract from the play. David and Kevin are the two brothers.

MOTHER	What're you so quiet about?
DAVID	Can I have a black shirt, mum?
KEVIN	Here we go.
DAVID	Shut up you!
KEVIN	Watch it!
DAVID	Watch it yourself!
MOTHER	You two!!
	(Silence)
	Why? Why do you want a black shirt?
DAVID	(Low) Cos. . . . I want one.
MOTHER	And you always get what you want?
DAVID	No.
MOTHER	Why then?
KEVIN	Cos everybody else's got one!
MOTHER	I didn't ask you.
DAVID	(Helplessly) Cos I. . . . just want one.
MOTHER	And you've got to be like everybody else, I suppose.
DAVID	No.
KEVIN	Yes.
DAVID	No.
MOTHER	Oh stop it, both of you. I can't be bothered with that now. Off to school, you'll be late.
	(Pause)
DAVID	(Persistent) Can I have one?
MOTHER	No.

DAVID	Why not?
MOTHER	It all costs money, that's why not. When I cough, three-penny bits don't drop out, you know.
DAVID	All our lot in the form've got them. (Kevin baas like a sheep)
MOTHER	I bought you both a new white one only the other week. I'm not made of money. School rules say white shirts, not black.
DAVID	It's not for school!
MOTHER	No need to raise your voices. Besides, you've got other shirts for best and for knocking around —
DAVID	It's not for knocking around in —
MOTHER	Then what's it for? Come on, tell me.
DAVID	I just *want* one.

From *Five Green Bottles* by Ray Jenkins

For discussion

1 Devise a scene to follow this.
2 What are the various reasons David might have for *not* saying why he wants the black shirt? How does this affect the scene?
3 How common is the situation in this scene? Has anything like this ever happened to you?
4 Devise the scene in which David gets the idea of wanting a black shirt.
5 What are the different ways in which the story might end?
  Could it have a tragic ending? a comic ending?

* * *

A House for Mr Biswas

For Mohun Biswas, success means a house of his own, but bad luck, bad health and a total lack of cash make it difficult for him to realise his dream. Eventually, against all the odds, he succeeds in raising a mortgage on a house — though it is not quite the house of his dreams:

> They discovered the staircase: unhidden by curtains, it was too plain. Mr Biswas discovered the absence of a back door. Shama discovered that two of the wooden pillars supporting the staircase landing were rotten, whittled away towards the bottom and green with damp. They all discovered that the staircase was dangerous. At every step it shook, and at the lightest breeze the sloping corrugated iron sheets rose in the middle and gave snaps which were like metallic sighs.

Shama did not complain. She only said, 'It look as though we will have to do a few repairs before we move.'. . . .

The drawingroom door could not open at all: it was pinned to the wall by two floorboards which had risen, pressing against each other, to make a miniature and even mountain range.

'Jerry-builder,' Mr Biswas said.

They discovered that nothing was faced and that the lattice work was everywhere uneven, and split in many places by nails which showed their large heads.

'Tout! Crook!'

They discovered that upstairs no door resembled any other, in shape, structure, colour or hinging. None fitted. One stood six inches off the floor, like the swingdoor of a bar.

'Nazi and blasted communist!'

The upper floor curved towards the centre and from downstairs they noted a corresponding bend in the two main beams. Shama thought that the floor curved because the inner verandah wall it supported was made of brick.

'We'll knock it down,' Shama said, 'and put a wood partition.'

'Knock it down!' Mr Biswas said. 'Be careful you don't knock down the house. For all we know it is that same wall which is keeping the whole damned thing standing.'

From *A House for Mr Biswas* by V S Naipaul, Deutsch 1961

For discussion

1 Mr Biswas has apparently been rather negligent in buying a house without previously first investigating its condition. Why is he likely to have done this? Have we ever done anything like this ourselves?
2 What sort of person is likely to have sold him the house in this condition? How might the sale have taken place?
3 Devise situations in which one person is able to sell something to another even though the commodity in question seems impossible to sell. Keep the situations plausible and varied.
4 How does the seller justify his action to himself or to others?
5 Families are constantly caught up in the business of buying things for one another — as in the previous extract from Ray Jenkins' play *Five Green Bottles*. Devise a story in which a family is united in its desire to buy *something* (such as a house in general) but unable to agree on the *particular* thing it is to buy. Then take part of the story to dramatise.

* * *

News story

Stop the jet — we want to get off!

The big jet to Brisbane was all set for take-off when mum and dad decided they didn't want to emigrate after all.

They had spent £1260 on tickets to fly to Australia with their four children, sold their house, and left the car in an airport car park to be picked up by relatives.

The Barlow family went through the Heathrow controls, through the security checks, settled themselves comfortably aboard and fastened their seat-belts. Then there was a hurried conversation and in the end it was mother who finally decided the issue. She said, 'I've made up my mind. I definitely don't want to go.'

According to airlines at Heathrow, there have been several cases of last-minute changes of heart about emigrating.

Later today a travel agent who made the Barlows' booking, said, 'They asked me to make another booking in a week's time, so they haven't abandoned their plans completely.'

For discussion

1. What is the possible background to this story? How might the family have made their plans for emigration?
2. What might happen next? Consider carefully the attitudes of different members of the family.
3. Dramatise the whole story.
4. We all change our minds — sometime or other — at the last moment. Can you remember such an incident?
5. Build up a biography for each member of the Barlow family, incorporating the events that follow the change of heart. Then set up situations in which each character meets, perhaps individually, different people to whom they narrate the whole story. Include neighbours, friends, relatives, etc.

* * *

Structured improvisation

There are four characters: Mrs Audrey Taylor, and her children, Jane, aged 13, and Barry, aged 12, and her old schoolfriend, Mrs Margaret Murray.

Instructions for ALL FOUR CHARACTERS: Mrs Taylor has told Jane and Barry to come home promptly from school, as she is expecting an old schoolfriend, Margaret Murray, to call round for tea, and she wants Margaret to meet her children. Mrs Taylor and Mrs Murray have not met for many years. After leaving school Mrs Murray emigrated to Australia, married and had a family. This is her first return visit to England, but the two women have remained in regular correspondence with each other. Mrs Murray has 'done well' — her husband is a very prosperous builder, and all her three children (two boys and a girl) are exceedingly clever and doing splendid things at school. Mrs Taylor has never been out of England. She married a boy she knew at school (Bert) who is now a foreman at a pressed steel works. Of her two children she tells people that Jane is good at everything at school, and Barry is a good boy and tries hard.

Instructions for BARRY: you have been given strict orders to make a good impression on Mrs Murray, and your mother is of the belief that you do not generally make a good impression at all. This is because your school reports tend to be 'critical' of your punctuality, your work, and your behaviour in general. In fact, of course, the reports are prejudiced against you — in other words they are written by teachers who just happen not to like you. Your particular interest in life is the group of folk singers to which you belong, and your particular ambition is to acquire your own guitar. You have no hope of ever saving enough money to do this, but are bringing a lot of pressure on your parents to buy you one for your next birthday. So you intend tactfully to 'blackmail' your mother into promising you a guitar in return for your making a good impression on Mrs Murray. But you are aware that Mrs Murray will probably be no fool, and you will have to answer her queries about yourself and your schooling, with great care (as well as with some misrepresentation where you think it is appropriate).

Instructions for JANE: you gather that Mrs Murray and your mother are not only old friends but also old rivals, and that quite a lot of envy flows between them. You find the thought of it very boring, but you expect to find the little tea party very interesting, *for two reasons*: (a) you have decided to amuse yourself, partly at your mother's expense, by exposing to Mrs Murray various aspects of the family's life that you know your mother is keen to hide. For instance, mother likes to say that Barry tries hard at school and is 'a good boy', but you — and he — know better. The only thing he's good at is singing dreary folk songs in some club he's joined. And mother likes to show off in all sorts of ways which you will try to expose, such as the home, the neighbourhood, dad's job, etc. You may even decide to pretend that you're in some kind of trouble. There is another reason: (b) a girl you know at school, has a penfriend in Australia, and as luck would have it, the penfriend goes to the same school as Mrs Murray's son, and he has just been expelled, apparently, for trying to blow up the school. He is in fact a notorious character and has often been in trouble. Your mother knows nothing of this, but you will choose a suitable moment over tea for testing Mrs Murray on the subject of her son, and then revealing to her what you know.

Instructions for MRS TAYLOR: although you are pleased to see Margaret again, your feelings are slightly mixed, for you are very envious of the money and success she achieved through her marriage. And you were always great rivals at school. You have told the two children to be on their best behaviour. Jane will find this easy, she is such a clever and sensible girl. But Barry will find it difficult, for he is in general mischievous, and often in trouble at school. His only enthusiasm is music — he wants a guitar so he can play at some music club or other. But of course, neither you nor your husband has money for such things. You do not wish Margaret to meet your husband. You think he would let the side down, and make a bad impression. You prefer to *describe* your husband (Bert) to her, and to do so in glowing terms so that she gets the very best impression of him. But you will make sure that she leaves before he gets home at six o'clock. (It is now just after four.)

Instructions for MRS MURRAY: your only reason for coming to see Mrs Taylor, and for keeping in correspondence with her, is that you knew her husband years ago, and liked him very much. And you are keen to see him again. You are a snob, and proud of the fact. You have done well in Australia: your husband is rich, and you have just divorced him (but keep this strictly to yourself) and on the allowance you get from him you will be able to travel round the world for as long as you choose. You might even take Mr Taylor with you. The only blot on your happiness is your son Leonard, who had recently been expelled from his school for some disgraceful action or other. You do not blame yourself for this, or even Leonard. You blame the schools and the teachers: they are so lax nowadays. At the tea party, your technique will be: (a) to display a great deal of charm and friendliness, and (b) to ask a great deal of questions, about the house, the children, their schooling, their father. . . You have some photos of your own home and family, and will show these with pride. Your aim is to stay as long as possible, in order to meet Mr Taylor (Bert) as if by chance when he eventually gets back from work. Mrs Taylor, as far as you know, has no idea that you ever made his acquaintance.

At the beginning of the scene: Mrs Taylor is preparing the tea, Mrs Murray has made herself at home, Barry arrives a few minutes later, and Jane arrives a few minutes after him.

7 Adventure

Some people spend all their lives looking for adventure. And finding it....

A meal with Robin Hood

And so Little John led the men from their hideout in the forest and out on to the highway. And the first people they saw were a small group of monks.
'Good day to you, good Holy Fathers,' cried Little John. The monks looked aprehensively at the tall monk who was leading them and said nothing.
'Good day to you, Sir,' said the leader. 'May the Lord bless you.'
'I'm sure He will,' said Little John, 'and right now He is blessing all five of you, for my master invites you to be his guests for dinner.'
'Your master is most kind,' said the leader of the monks. 'And may we know your master's name?'
'Robin Hood is our master,' said Little John. 'And no man in England has ever dared refuse his invitation.'
'Why should we refuse?' said the monk. 'My brothers here are hungry, and your master's invitation is most welcome.'
'Well, they look more scared than hungry,' said Little John.
'Not scared,' said the monk. 'Just lost in prayer.'
'They certainly don't look as if they're praying,' said Little John, whereupon all the monks began to pray out loud and call upon the good Lord to protect them from robbers and outlaws.
'And now you can lead us to your master,' said the leader. 'I have always wanted to meet your good Robin Hood.'
And with that they came to the hideout and Robin stepped forward to greet his guests.
'Good monks, you are most welcome,' he said. 'As you can see, my simple meal is good and wholesome. And though we shoot the King's deer to provide meat for our table, the King will never miss it.'
The monks crossed themselves hastily.
'You are most kind,' said the leader. And he led the company in prayers before they started on their meal. Robin and all the men were amused to see how heartily the monks proceeded to eat. Then, raising his

goblet filled with wine, the leader of the monks cried out: 'And now I propose a toast. Gentlemen, I call on you to be upstanding with me and drink to the health of — ' there was a pause, and then the monk continued, 'and drink to the health of His Gracious Majesty, King Richard of England.' There was another pause.

'We are not great lovers of the King, as you well know, Sir,' said Robin Hood angrily.

From *Stories for Improvisation* by Peter Chilver, based on a
a medieval ballad, *The Gest of Robin Hood*

For discussion

1 What might happen next? Consider carefully all the possible developments in the story. Perhaps choose the one that an audience is least likely to expect, and improvise it.
2 Dramatise the story as a piece of *group story-telling,* with different members of the group taking up the narrative, and with various scenes being acted out.
3 Can you think of other adventure stories with episodes like this? Tell them to the class.
4 Can you think of any times in your own lives when you have in effect, set yourself up as a Robin Hood — someone who takes the law into his own hands in order to put wrong to right?
5 In this story, and in the versions of it that you have talked about or improvised, what are the different characters that could be given to Robin Hood? How might *different* people see his character? (For instance, how might those in power or authority? or *former* members of his band of outlaws?)

* * *

Sometimes, people hit upon adventure accidentally. As in this news story:

> *Boy discovers microfilm in his Polish shoelaces*
> Detectives took three pairs of shoes from a shop in Prestatyn, Denbighshire, today, after a boy had found strips of microfilm in his shoelaces. They advised the shop-owner to remove the rest of the Polish-made stock from the counter and keep it out of sight.
> Mrs Sheila Howie, of Bangor Crescent, Prestatyn, bought a pair of the shoes a fortnight ago for £3.49 at the local brance of Stead and Simpson. A few days later her son, William, aged 13, was playing with a metal clasp on one of the laces when he peeled

Adventure

off two strips of microfilm. He found similar film on each of the other three ends of the laces.

Mrs Howie said: 'He showed me the pieces and I said, Don't be silly. You have been watching too much television.'

Later she decided to tell the police. Detectives took away the film and a few days later returned with an enlargement from one film. It showed three men wearing soft canvas hats, walking apparently unaware that they were being photographed. The policeman, Mrs Howie said, told her that the films would be sent to M16.

Mr Alan Brown, manager of the shoe shop, said the consignment came from the head office in Leicester. 'I have got seven and a half dozen pairs of Polish shoes here,' he said. 'I shall be checking through the lot to see if there is any more film on any of them. I have certainly never heard of film being used on laces before.'

A police officer at Prestatyn divisional headquarters said: 'Our investigations are still continuing and we cannot say any more at the moment.'

Later Mrs Howie and Mr Brown said the police had advised them not to say anything further.

For discussion

1 What might be happening?
2 What might happen next?
3 Has anything like this ever happened to any of us?
4 Dramatise the story. Perhaps use a narrator to link different scenes.

* * *

And there are even ways of *avoiding adventure* if you so wish. In June 1977 the Italian police were so put upon by the kidnappings of rich business men or members of their family (who were then held up for ransom) that they published a list of seven tips on how to avoid becoming the next victim:

How not to be kidnapped

1 Do not go on foot, and make sure someone is with you when you walk to or from your car.
2 Make sure that your car always has plenty of petrol so that you do not have to stop at a petrol station.
3 Have bullet-proof windows installed in your car, and an ear-splitting horn to give the alarm in case of danger.
4 If you see a road accident, do not slow down or get out. It may be

a trap. Drive on and telephone the police.
5 Only have trusted employees around you in your office, factory or home.
6 Have your children escorted everywhere they go. Tell the school to check with the family if someone phones asking for them to be let out early.
7 If you live in an isolated spot, have guard dogs, and light up the house and garden at night.

If however, you are still kidnapped, do not put up a fight or you will be hurt. Try to gather as many clues as you can as to your captors and your whereabouts.

For discussion
1 Do you think the list is practical? Do you think it is comprehensive? Would you add to it?
2 The implication is that those who follow the advice may still be kidnapped. Devise a story in which this happens.
3 After you have devised the story, give each character a full biography. Then devise situations in which each character in turn can be interviewed by the whole class acting as, say, press reporters, police, lawyers, etc.

* * *

In the following news story, a group of youngsters unintentionally get involved in an adventure, and handle the situation very coolly and calmly:

Desert island rescue
Six youths from the Pacific Island of Tonga, reported missing nine months ago when their rowing boat disappeared on a fishing trip, have been found alive and well on a deserted island — two thousand miles from home. Their parents and friends had given them up for dead.

The youths told reporters they had lived happily together on the island. They had kept a regular system of watches to look out for passing ships. They had devised their own musical instruments; had kept diaries on tree trunks; and lived well by eating the fish which they caught in large numbers.

They were pleased to be home, but they all agreed they would be happy to do it again.

For discussion
1 Dramatise the story.
2 Now re-dramatise the story, changing your characters. Either change

the parts round, or find a different sort of person to represent. (You might change for instance, from a very relaxed to a very nervous person.)
3 Have you ever in any way been caught up in an adventure like this?
4 What opportunities exist for people to have 'adventures' in the everyday world? Do you prefer life to offer such opportunities or not?

* * *

And finally an instance of people coming together in the vague expectation of something adventurous happening, but not quite able (or keen enough, perhaps) actually to cause something to happen. The following extract is from *Folk Devils and Moral Panic* by Stanley Cohen, in which the author looks at the ways 'mods' and 'rockers' gathered at seaside resorts not so much to make trouble, but because the newspapers and the TV commentators were *predicting* that there would be trouble. The results were sometimes disappointing for all concerned:

> Their aim was excitement, but for most of the time nothing happened and so the dominant feelings were boredom, a sense of drifting aimlessness and lack of any specific plans. The following conversation, overheard between two fifteen-year-old girls huddled together on a windswept Brighton beach, conveys something of this tone:
> *First girl:* What's the time?
> *Second girl:* Three o'clock.
> *First:* Blimey, we don't have to sit around here for another three hours, do we?
> *Second:* We could get a train before.
> *First:* Well, but you never know.
> Another time, I asked an Eltham boy whether he was enjoying himself. 'Not really.' Why did he come then, when this was all he knew he could find? 'There's nothing doing in London.' But what is there doing anywhere that you'd like to do? 'Well, if you put it like that, there isnt.'.....
> This boredom was accompanied though by the perpetual hope that something would happen; after all, 'You never know.'
> Was Brighton what you expected?
> Well, I didn't expect anything, I don't think.
> No?
> Well, you know, I just thought I'd see what was happening, and if things turned out right, then we'd have a ball, wouldn't we?
> It is clear that for 'things to turn out right' would mean that there would be trouble between Mods and Rockers, baiting of the police,

throwing some girls into the sea, or 'finding a bird'. If these things happened one would 'Have a ball'; there was no specific plan in coming down other than to take part in or to watch any sign of fun.

From *Folk Devils and Moral Panic* by Stanley Cohen, MacGibbon and Kee 1972

For discussion
1 Imagine that all of you are on the beach at just such a time, and that one of you goes round to interview the others.
2 Like the characters mentioned in the extract, you are all gathering and *waiting*. Improvise different conversations.
3 Have you ever been caught up in such a scene? What caused you to take part? What do you remember of it? Do you think *everyone* does at *some* time?
4 Devise a structured improvisation on the theme of *adventure*. Follow the same pattern as in the structured improvisations in other sections of this book:
   Choose a limited number of characters, perhaps only two;
   devise a situation which brings them together;
   give them specific characters;
   give the two characters some 'data' which they will know about each other eg. they might know they are both candidates for the same job;
   write down the data;
   do the same with the characters individually, providing them with some kind of intention which will carry them into the scene, something they want;
   having written down all the sets of instructions,
      check them through, then find your actors and set up the scene.
Afterwards, discuss the way the scene developed, and how you expected it to develop, and then perhaps have a shot at writing the scene, in dialogue-form.

8 Thief

Begin with a news story:

> Two sisters aged 13 and 14 stole a total of £400 from pensioners in Birmingham. They used various tricks in a series of thefts in the Sparkhill area, which the police could not solve.
> Detective Constable Kevin Phillips told the Birmingham Juvenile Court yesterday, that a group of children would throw a ball into a garden and one of them would knock on the door of the house and ask for it back.
> While the occupier was looking for the ball one of the group would go into the house and steal whatever they could find.
> A breakthrough was made when the younger sister was detained after further raids.
> In court she admitted stealing a purse containing £80 and another containing £50, and asked for eleven other offences to be considered. Her sister admitted her involvement in some of these.
> Several of their victims were very elderly people, and none of the money has been recovered.
> Both girls were remanded in care until November, for reports from psychologists and welfare officers.

For discussion
1 How, if at all, would you punish the girls?
2 Why do people do such things?
3 Would you say that most of us are thieves, at some time or other, or only a minority of us?
4 Have you ever stolen? or been the victim of a theft? Improvise the incident.
5 Is it worse to steal from some people than from others?
6 Is theft ever justified?

* * *

Moll Flanders
In Daniel Defoe's novel *Moll Flanders*, first published in 1722, the heroine survives terrible misfortune and poverty, mainly through her talent for different kinds of thieving. In this scene, quite early in her career, when already a grown woman, she steals from a small child:

Going through Aldersgate Street, there was a pretty little child had been at a dancing school and was agoing home all alone. And like a true devil, I set upon this innocent creature. I talked to it and it talked to me, and I took it by the hand and led it along till I came to a paved alley that goes into Bartholomew Close, and I led it in there. The child said, that was not its way home. I said, 'Yes my dear, it is. I'll show you the way home.' The child had a little necklace on of gold beads and I had my eye upon that, and in the dark of the alley I stooped, pretending to mend the child's clog that was loose, and took off her necklace and the child never felt it, and so led the child on again. Here I say the devil put me upon killing the child in the dark alley, that it might not cry, but the very thought frightened me so that I was ready to drop down. But I turned the child about, and bade it to go back again, for that was not its way home. The child said, so she would. . . . . Poverty hardened my heart, and my own necessities made me regardless of anything. The last affair left no great concern upon me, for as I did the poor child no harm, I only thought I had given the parents a just reproof for their negligence in leaving the poor lamb to come home by herself, and it would teach them to take more care another time.

From *Moll Flanders* by Daniel Defoe

For discussion
1. Moll Flanders gives a good reason for her theft. Would you accept this? Would this excuse her from punishment?
2. What similarities are there between the case of Moll Flanders, and that of the schoolgirls who stole from old people? What differences?
3. Improvise the scene between Moll and the girl. How might the girl herself narrate what happened (perhaps to her parents)? Compare the scene with Fagin's lesson for Oliver Twist in the art of picking pockets.
4. What is the evidence that Moll is a good girl at heart? (Or is she?)
5. Have you yourself ever done anything you know to be wrong, but where circumstances compelled you to do it? And — Did the circumstances really compel you? or are they just an excuse? (Are they an excuse perhaps, in the case or Moll Flanders?)

* * *

Kleptomaniacs

Some people cannot stop stealing. They're addicted to it. They're kleptomaniacs. The following extract is a true story, taken from the memoirs of Jessica Mitford, where she recalls a childhood spent not at school (her parents refused to send her or her sisters) but in the company of a succession of private governesses. Most of the governesses fled because they were terrified of the sisters. But one of them was popular, and she stayed. She was a kleptomaniac, and, unknown to the girls' parents, she took them on stealing-expeditions:

> Miss Bunting's main contribution to our education was to teach a little mild shop-lifting. Miss Bunting was a dear little round giggly woman, shaped like a Toby jug, with a carefree and unorthodox approach to life that we found most attractive. My sister Boud towered over her and sometimes scooped her up and put her, squealing, on the schoolroom piano.
> We made occasional trips to Oxford. 'Like to try a little jiggery-pokery, children?' Miss Bunting suggested. There were two main methods: the shopping-bag method, in which an accomplice was needed, was used for larger items. The accomplice undertook to distract the shop-lady while the lifter, or jiggery-poker in Miss Bunting's idiom, stuffed her bag with books, underclothes or boxes of chocolates, depending on the wares of the particular store. The dropped-hanky method was suitable for lipsticks or small pieces of jewellery. Miss Bunting in her governessy beige coat and gloves, Boud and I in matching panama straw hats, would strut haughtily past the sales people to seek the safety of Fuller's Tea Room, where we would gleefully take stock of the day's haul over cups of steaming hot chocolate.
> Miss Bunting was very relaxed about lessons. Only when she heard my mother's distinctive tread approaching the schoolroom did she signal us to buckle down to work. She knew nothing and cared less about Algebra, Latin or the parts of the bean, and needless to say we liked her much better than any of her predecessors. We did all we could to make life tolerably attractive for her, with the result that she stayed on for some years.
>
> From *Hons and Rebels* by Jessica Mitford, Gollancz 1960

For discussion
1 Do you regard Miss Bunting's expeditions as serious? How do you think she should be punished if caught? Should the girls also be punished? How?
2 Imagine that the parents found out what was happening. Improvise the scene.
3 What might have happened if the girls had been different people? (Suppose one of the sisters had been shocked.)
4 Improvise scenes with previous governesses.
5 Improvise the scene where Miss Bunting is interviewed for the job.

* * *

Thief

Structured improvisation

This improvisation involves *the whole class,* who act together as a court of inquiry, plus *two boys and two girls* as individual characters — Kay, Laura, Jerry, Mike.

Instructions for EVERYONE: the whole class have recently gone on a coach outing to the Science Museum in London (or to some other more likely place, if needs be), with yourself as the teacher in charge. On the way there it was widely known that Kay had with her a postal order for £10 given to her that morning as a birthday present from her mother and father. When the class left the coach to go into the Museum, Kay left the Postal Order in her handbag on the coach, and the coach was locked at this time. All the class were under instructions to keep together while going round the Museum, and not to wander away. But Laura and Mike disappeared, together, and so did Jerry. They were all three late getting back to the coach. Jerry was half an hour late, and Laura and Mike were an hour late. They were severely reprimanded for this by the teacher. The coach then started off on the journey home, and about fifteen minutes later Kay screamed out that she had lost her Postal Order: somebody had stolen it. Laura and Mike were sitting in front of Kay, and Jerry was behind her. Kay accused all three of them, loudly and hysterically. To calm her down, you, the teacher, decided to search the jackets of the two boys, not believing for one moment that you would find the Order. To your surprise you immediately found it in the inside pocket of Jerry's jacket. Jerry protested his innocence, but the next day you had no option but to report the whole matter to the Headmaster. At the same time, Jerry's father came up to the school to tell the Head that, to his belief, Jerry had been wrongly accused. The Head asks you and the class to conduct your own inquiry into the matter and to report back to him.

The class will question each of the four in turn, and will then vote on their decision.

Individual instructions for JERRY *(alone):* you are saving money to buy a bike, and are doing a newspaper round to help you. When you left the coach to go into the Museum, you left your coat on the coach: it was a warm day. You dislike Laura and Mike, and think they probably stole the money order themselves and planted it on you when the other girl, Kay, started screaming. Your reason for coming back to the coach so late was that you had wandered over to the Natural History Museum, which is nearby, and in fact you are more interested in biology and natural history than in science. You are a very good, very moral young man, and if your father suddenly decides that you did actually steal the money, you think it's very possible that he will kill you. You hope to be able to cast the blame onto Laura or Mike or both.

Individual instructions for KAY *(alone):* you have never been in trouble of any kind in your entire life. You are a *very* good girl. But last term you happened to lose some money (a few pounds in cash) and a friend told you that Jerry had stolen it. You had no evidence to prove it, but you've had it in for Jerry ever since. On this occasion, you yourself planted the money in Jerry's jacket when you realised that he was late coming back to the coach. You only meant it as a sort of joke, intending to tell the truth eventually. But now the whole business has got out of hand, and it is too late to do anything about it. Besides, you still think that Jerry stole the money last term, so you think it's quite fair that he should be punished this term for something he has not done. You also dislike Mike and Laura — which is why you called out their names as well as Jerry's when you 'discovered' that the Postal Order was missing. On no account are you to tell the truth at the inquiry. It would make you look a fool. And it would get you into trouble.

Individual instructions for MIKE *(alone):* you have been in trouble once or twice before, when people have accused you of stealing things, but you have never been found officially guilty. In fact you are something of a thief, but are careful to leave no evidence. You dislike Jerry, considering him a creep, a weed, etc. You like all girls, and Laura in particular. You feel chivalrous towards almost every girl in the class, including Kay. You have thought a lot about what happened on the coach, and your private views are: (i) that Jerry is too much of a coward to dare to steal anything from anybody; (ii) that whoever stole the PO, eventually planted it on Jerry, to avoid being found out; (iii) that it must have been somebody who hates Jerry as much as you do; and (iv) the only person who fits that description is Kay herself. But you will on no account say anything to anybody that indicates your suspicions. At the same time, you will not allow any further suspicion to fall on yourself.

Individual instructions for LAURA *(alone):* you are very fond of Mike, but you know that he is rather inclined to steal things every now and then. So your guess is that on this occasion it is Mike who stole the PO, and then concealed it in Jerry's jacket. But you wish at all cost to save Mike from conviction, from being found guilty. So your plan is to pretend that you saw Jerry take the money as you were coming back into the coach. You will have to think carefully, and give your evidence with great 'sincerity', and on no account are you to reveal the truth.

At the Inquiry members of the class will ask such questions of the individual characters as they think appropriate. They will try to draw out as much as possible in the way of material evidence about who did what and why. They will then vote on the question: is there any fair evidence to indicate who took the Postal Order, and if so, who took it?

9 Telling Tales

Schoolboy paid out £234 to blackmailer
A boy of 15 who obtained £234 from a boy of 14 by threatening to tell his father that he had bought a motor-scooter, was fined £50 at Leeds juvenile court yesterday. He admitted demanding money with menaces.

The chairman of the magistrates told the boy that the offence was despicable. 'It is one of the worst offences we can imagine,' he said.

For discussion

1 This is a very short and simple story. What do you think has actually happened? What sort of boys have been involved? And how is the blackmailer likely to have worked?
2 Improvise the blackmail and the events leading up to it.
3 Improvise sequences to show the home-life of both the boys.
4 What are the various ways in which the truth may have come to life?
5 The magistrate spoke of it as 'one of the worst offences we can imagine'. Would you agree? If not, why do you think the magistrate called it this?
6 How would you punish the offender in such a case? Would you punish him at all? What would you expect to achieve by the punishment?
7 Have you ever been blackmailed? Or have you ever blackmailed anyone?

* * *

The blackmail case became public and landed the blackmailer (and perhaps the blackmail victim) in trouble. The following is in some respect similar, and is taken from a girl's account in the classroom of how she also was trapped in a parallel predicament:

> My dad was very ill, and in the lunch-hour that day my mum gave me a pound to go over to the shops and buy him some cigarettes — it was to cheer him up, she said. My dad likes smoking, even when he's ill. So I went to the shops like she said, but on the way there I thought how I'd like to spend the money on myself. There was a magazine I wanted to buy. I know it was mean of me, but what I did, I bought

the magazine and hid it away and told my mum that a gang of boys had set on me and I'd lost the pound somehow, in the scramble. My mum believed me.

Now what happened next, was that one of my friends — well, his mum knew my mum, and they were speaking, and my mum told his mum about the gang and the missing pound. His mum must have told it to him, and then he remembered that he's seen me in the shop buying my magazine, and he added one and one together, and he guessed what had happened. So he came up to me and said that I'd have to pay him a pound or he'd tell on me.

I was scared stiff, because I didn't have a pound to give him, and I knew my mum would never forgive me if she knew what I'd done. Besides, my dad was still very ill, and that made it even worse....

For discussion
1 What would you have done?
2 What are the various possible ways of resolving the dilemma? Which are most most likely to lead to further trouble? and which are most likely to bring no trouble at all?
3 Improvise the story.
4 Re-improvise, changing your characters around, so that the blackmailer becomes the blackmailed, etc. Now introduce an entirely new character.

* * *

The folktale

The French writer *Marcel Eliade* tells of an anthropologist (one who studies the life of primitive societies) who was collecting folk-tales from a very remote rural people in southern Europe. He was told the story of a girl whose intended spouse was killed by a jealous spirit on the very eve of her marriage. The spirit wanted the husband for herself, and while he was bringing his flock of sheep down from the mountainside the spirit lured him to a great height and led him to his death. He was also told that this was an entirely true story, and — not only that — the girl herself was still alive, though now an old spinster. She had moved from the village to another one on the other side of the mountain. So the anthropologist decided to go and see her, and check the story with her. But when he heard the story from her it was all rather different. Her lover had indeed fallen to his death the day before the marriage, but it had been an accident, and such accidents were not uncommon on mountainsides. She had heard of no jealous spirits, nor did she believe in such things. Nor was she old and grey. (The incident is told more fully in *The Myth of the Eternal Return* by Marcel Eliade.)

For discussion
1 How do stories come to be changed as they pass around from teller to teller? Are the changes deliberate?
2 When do you know whether to believe the stories you hear?
3 Think of something interesting that you have heard, or that you have been involved in. Tell it to the person next to you. Then ask that person to tell it to someone else. Now have the story related back to you, or back to the class. What has happened to the story?
4 Can you think of any important occasions when a tale has been changed in the telling, and with important consequences? (There might be incidents in fiction or in history as well as in your own life.)
5 Generally speaking, even when we are trying very hard to tell the truth, the whole truth, and nothing but the truth, there are certain limits to what we can remember. Think of an incident which you remember vividly, and tell it to the class or group. Now get them to ask you questions about it, and to carry on doing so until either they get you to contradict yourself, or discover important matters which you do not know or have forgotten.
6 If possible, do the same as in (5), but find an incident which two or more of you have witnessed or taken part in. (This might be an incident from a TV newscast, or from a film etc.) Again, get the others to question all of you until you reach contradictions or limitations in your accounts of what happened.

* * *

Structured improvisation (involving the whole class)

There are three characters, three schoolboys, Peter, Geoff and Alan.
Instructions for ALL THREE: you have been on an outward bound expedition to the Yorkshire moors, as part of the Duke of Edinburgh's Award Scheme. You were all keen to do well on the expedition, and having done well on slightly less ambitious projects earlier in the year, this represented the greatest challenge for you. You know each other well, and get along together reasonably well. *Peter* is a star pupil in every way, good at games, at PE, and at all his work in school. Everybody thinks highly of him. *Geoff* is brilliant at his school-work, but is widely thought of as rather weedy and nervous. *Alan* is not very good at anything, and is often in trouble. But he has done very well at the various projects for the earlier stages of the Award Scheme. All three of you went on the moors expedition with a teacher (Mr Pallen) and three other schoolboys.

As part of the expedition, the three of you together had to build a raft, and negotiate the raft down a short stretch of river. You built the raft successfully, and then took it down the river. (The others meanwhile were doing the same thing at another part of the river.) While going down the river on the raft, there was an accident, and the raft capsized. *Peter* swam to the riverbank. *Geoff* nearly drowned, called for help, and was saved by *Alan*, who holds a life-saving certificate. And the raft was lost. The Award was lost also, for the failure of the raft escapade, meant that the three of you are disqualified from the final stages of the Scheme.

In reporting the incident to Mr Pallen, the three of you gave conflicting accounts of what happened. *Peter* said that Alan caused the accident deliberately, by fooling about and showing off. *Geoff* said that Peter caused it, by 'picking on' Alan and trying to provoke him into a fight. And *Alan* said that it was nobody's fault, just a pure accident: suddenly the raft went off balance for no apparent reason.

Mr Pallen has decided that no candidate for the Award (plus the opportunity to be presented to the Duke of Edinburgh in person) should be failed because of the misbehaviour of any other candidate, and so he will hold an inquiry at which each of the three boys will be closely questioned, in turn, about the events on the raft. *The whole class* will sit as the inquiry-team.

NB. Prior to the accident on the raft, all three boys were regarded as good contestants for the Award.

Individual instructions for PETER *(alone):* you do not dislike Alan, but you have always regarded him as somewhat unreliable. His record at school shows that. Teachers often find him intolerable. He said several times on the expedition, that the whole thing was a joke, not to be taken seriously. He told you (privately) that it would be fun if all of you failed at at the final hurdle, as it were, to qualify for the Award. You had, and still have, every intention of qualifying for it. What happened was very simple. While you were going down the river on the raft, Alan started playing games, saying that rafts were marvellous places to be, because anyone on a raft could upset (literally) everyone else, just by moving into the wrong position. Geoff then started to panic. He is a very nervous youth, and you do not understand why he should have entered the Scheme in the first place. He then shouted that he was not able to swim, or at least not sure that he could swim in this particular river. In shouting about and getting very nervous, Geoff himself changed position on the raft and caused the raft to capsize. Alan immediately went to rescue Geoff, and you swam to the bank. Now, you know that Geoff is technically to blame, but you are aware that in reality it is Alan who caused the trouble. You will tell the truth, but will place the blame securely where it lies.

Instrucitons for GEOFF *(alone):* you have hated the Scheme, and the expedition to the Moors. You only did it to please your father, who has promised you a holiday in America if you qualify for the top prize in the Award Scheme. What happened on the raft was very simple: Alan is always very humorous, and he started to make jokes about the raft capsizing. Peter is entirely humourless, and wouldn't recognise a joke to save his life, and he became very bossy and told Alan to behave himself. In effect, the conflict became so intense between the two, that anyone with less good humour and good sense than Alan would have punched Peter there and then, and thrown him into the river. In fact, Peter moved towards Alan, *perhaps* to hit him, and capsized the raft. You became slightly alarmed, because the current was strong and were not sure if your swimming was good enough to keep you going, but Alan very kindly helped you to swim to the bank. Peter meanwhile, had no interest in anyone's safety but his own, and had swum to the bank and was already shouting out that he would report both of you to Mr Pallen. It is Peter who caused the trouble, and you will make this entirely clear at the inquiry.

Instructions for ALAN *(alone):* you have enjoyed the expedition, and the Scheme, but you think that some people take it rather too seriously. You do not dislike either Geoff or Peter, but find both of them rather solemn. You have said as much to both of them on various occasions. What happened on the raft was very simple: you tried to make a few jokes, and talked about how easy it would be to capsize the raft. Peter became very severe about this, and reminded you of your duties 'to the team' and 'to the spirit of the Duke of Edinburgh's Award Scheme'. Geoff became very nervous, crying out that the raft must on no account capsize, because he wasn't sure that he would be strong enough to swim against the current. You then tried to 'cool it', but in fact Geoff became more and more upset, and Peter became more aggressive, and in a moment of confusion, one or other of them (you *think* it was Peter) moved impulsively on the raft and capsized it. Geoff started screaming for help, you at once went to his rescue and demonstrated your skills as a lifesaver, and brought him safely to shore. As far as you are concerned: (a) the accident was just an accident. It was *not* your fault. And (b) it is unfair to say it was *anyone's* fault. Possibly Peter moved in such a way as to capsize the raft, possibly (but less likely) it was Geoff who did this. But neither intended to do it. And neither was acting foolishly or recklessly.

The class will inquire into the incident, and try to determine what actually happened, and whether anyone was actually to blame.

10 The Gang

In one way or another, we all belong to gangs. They not only give us security and identity, they also keep others out: they are exclusive. *George Orwell's* story describes a boy's attempts to get in with his brother's gang.

My brother Joe got in with a tough gang of boys who called themselves the Black Hand. The leader was Sid Lovegrove, the saddler's younger son, who was thirteen, and there were two other shopkeepers' sons, an errand boy from the brewery, and two farm lads who sometimes managed to cut work and go off with the gang for a couple of hours. The farm lads were great lumps bursting out of corduroy breeches, with very broad accents and rather looked down on by the rest of the gang, but they were tolerated because they knew twice as much about animals as any of the others. One of them, nicknamed Ginger, would even catch a rabbit in his hands occasionally. If he saw one lying in the grass he used to fling himself on it like a spread-eagle. The gang had a secret password and an 'ordeal' which included cutting your finger and eating an earthworm, and they gave themselves out to be frightful desperadoes. Certainly they managed to make a nuisance of themselves, broke windows, chased cows, tore the knockers off doors, and stole fruit by the hundredweight. Sometimes in winter they manage to borrow a couple of ferrets and go ratting, when the farmers would let them. Of course I was wild to join the Black Hand, but Joe always choked me off and said they didn't want any blasted kids hanging around. It was the thought of going fishing that really appealed to me. At eight years old I hadn't yet been fishing, except with a penny net, with which you can sometimes catch a stickle-bat. Mother was always terrified of letting us go anywhere near water. She forbade fishing, in the way in which parents in those days forbade almost anything, and I hadn't yet grasped that grownups can't see around corners. But the thought of fishing sent me wild with excitement. . . .

One morning I knew that Joe was going to cut school and go out fishing, and I made up my mind to follow. In some way, Joe guessed what I was thinking about, and he started on me while we were dressing.

'Now then, young George! Don't you get thinking you're coming with the gang today. You stay back home.'
'No, I didn't. I didn't think nothing about it.'
'Yes you did. You thought you were coming with the gang.'
'No, I didn't!'
'Yes, you did!'
'No, I didn't!'
'Yes, you did! You stay back home. We don't want any bloody kids along.'

Joe had just learned the word 'bloody' and was always using it. Father overheard him once, and swore that he'd thrash the life out of Joe, but as usual he didn't do so. After breakfast Joe started off on his bike, with his satchel and his Grammar School cap, five minutes early as he always did when he meant to cut school, and when it was time for me to leave for my school I sneaked off and hid in the lane behind the allotments. I knew the gang were going to the pond at the Mill Farm, and I was going to follow them if they murdered me for it.

From *Coming up for Air* by George Orwell, Gollancz 1945
Reprinted by permission of Mrs Sonia Bronwell Orwell

For discussion
1 Devise a sequel to the story.
2 Have you ever been in a similar situation, wanting to join a group from which you are strictly excluded? What happened?
3 Improvise either the story by Orwell, extending it as you wish, or one of your own experiences.
4 Why do people form gangs? What different sorts of gangs are there?
5 How do gangs find leaders? Do all gangs have leaders?

* * *

The very word 'gang' is usually used in a pejorative or critical sense, to imply that the members of the gang should never have got together in the first place. (And of course 'gangsters' are automatically law-breakers, or they would never be called gangsters!)

The following *news story* is a fairly typical use of the word 'gang':

Gang mugs park boy for 50p
A gang of teenagers forced money out of a local schoolboy by putting a knife to each cheek and a dog chain round his neck, in the Southchurch Park on Sunday afternoon. And people walking by ignored 13-year-old Jimmy Valentine's terrifying ordeal.

Jimmy's mother said: 'The police say they've never had an incident like this in Southchurch Park before. I am really worried. I don't quite know what to do. I can't stop him going out, but I've asked him not to go to Southchurch Park again.'

Jimmy said: 'I was really frightened. They looked really dangerous. They asked my friends and me if we had change of 5p and we said we hadn't. Then they asked how much money I had, and by then they were looking down my pockets.'

With the chain round his neck, and the knives being prodded in his body and face, Jimmy gave up his 50p, which included his bus fare home.

'There were a lot of people walking by but they took no notice,' Jimmy said.

For discussion

1 Why do such things happen? Is there any way of avoiding them?
2 Have such things ever happened to you?
3 How, if at all, would you punish the members of the gang?
4 Why did the people passing by do nothing to help?
5 Set up an inquiry at which all the various characters give their explanation of what happened. Include the members of the gang, Jimmy, and his friends, and also passersby.

* * *

Sometimes, 'gangs' are created by those in power as a means of organising the people underneath them. (Then they are not usually called gangs, of course.) For example, in the USSR, small groups of pupils are elected (by their fellow classmates) to act as disciplinary boards whose job it is to keep an eye on everyone's work and behaviour and to impose various measures or penalties when people fall out of line:

Vova neglects his maths

It was Friday noon and the five elected officers of the soviet (council) of Class 5-B were having their weekly meeting to evaluate each pupil. Normally no adult was present. The procedure required rating each class member on a scale of 1 to 5 on the basis of all aspects of his behaviour: school grades, cleanliness, execution of civic duties, athletics, etc. The final mark was written on a slip of paper to be given to each child, who in turn had to take it home and have it acknowledged by a parent's signature.

The young people took their responsibilities very seriously. They were discussing Sasha, editor of the class newspaper. Lyolya, the class commander, asked for a judgment. One of the youngsters offered the opinion that while the recent issues were good, there had been little originality, no new feature articles. 'Well then, let's give him a 4 instead of a 5,' proposed another. 'It may jack him up a bit.'

The next case was more difficult. A month ago, Vova had been warned that he was doing poorly in arithmetic and pulling down the class. There had been no improvement.

After some discussion, Lyolya proposed: 'I think this problem is serious enough to require action by the entire collective. We can call a special meeting for this afternoon.'

At the class meeting (ie the entire collective) Vova, a handsome lad in a white shirt, is called forward and asked what he did yesterday upon returning home from school.

'As always, I cleaned house so that Mother wouldn't have to do it when she got home. Then I did my homework.'

'What subjects?'

'English, history, some drawings.'

As no mention is made of math, the class officers exchange significant looks. In a stern voice, Chairman Lyolya reminds him, 'A month ago, you were warned to work hard on your maths, and now you don't even mention it.'

Vova: 'I didn't have any maths homework that night.'

Voice from the class: 'You should have studied it any way.'

Lyolya asks the class for recommendations. After some discussion a girl with a blue hair ribbon asks for the floor.

'I propose that we designate two of our classmates to supervise Vova as he does his maths homework every night and give him help as needed.'

Vova objects: 'I don't need them. I can do it by myself. I promise.'

But Lyolya is not impressed. Turning to Vova she says, quietly:

'We have seen what you do by yourself. Now two of your classmates will work with you and when *they* say you are ready to work alone, we'll believe it.'

From *Two Worlds of Childhood* by Urie Bronfenbrenner, Allen and Unwin 1971

For discussion

1 What do you think of such a way of running a class and of supervising children's work?
2 What do you think the adult society sees as its virtue? Why do you think we do not, in general, have such a system here?
3 Improvise the scene (or scenes) where Vova undertakes his maths homework, under supervision.
4 What might be the reaction of Vova's parents?

5 Imagine that you wished to introduce such a system in your own class. How would you persuade others (including the teachers) of its advantages?
6 Have you ever been caught up in a similar situation? (ie. where you were being judged by your own fellows and peer group.)
7 Devise a situation where the Russian system is working in your school and the soviet/council meets to review the pupils' weekly progress.

* * *

Devise a structured improvisation on the theme of *the gang*. You might devise this in groups, and then give the instructions to each other's groups to perform. Perhaps take as your basic idea, the outsider trying to be admitted to a gang, with one outsider, and three gang members. See what different motives you can find for the outsider wishing to get in, and how you can vary the reasons which will lead the three to admit the newcomer or leave him/her out. The centre of the drama would then be the outsider presenting his/her case, and the other three deciding upon it.

11 Lies

West Point cadet accused of telling lies

West Point cadet Steven Verr has been accused of telling a lie to explain why he was found crying outside a mess hall last year. Cadet Verr has in turn accused West Point of persecuting him.

West Point's honour code, which is strictly enforced, states: 'A cadet will not lie, steal or cheat, or tolerate those who do.' Cadet Verr was deemed to have broken this and was transferred to transient barracks, a form of solitary confinement, while his case was investigated.

This happened last year. Since then he has made a number of charges alleging beatings and harrassment, having his mail and property stolen, being allowed to fall at gymnasium exercises, and undergoing a threatening psychiatric examination.

His case was taken up by one of the instructors, Captain Arthur Lincoln, a lecturer in law at West Point. Two weeks ago he called for a thorough investigation, and together with nine other Army lawyers wrote to the Secretary of the Army in Washington.

Last week, Captain Lincoln was aked to put in for reassignment elsewhere.

For discussion

1 The story given no indication of why Cadet Verr was crying outside the mess hall. What are the various possibilities?
2 In a case like this, where do your sympathies lie? And why? Do you feel sorry, for instance, for the Cadet? Or for the officer who tries to help him and then gets moved elsewhere? For the authorities at West Point?
3 Does the honour code at West Point strike you as a good one? Would you like it introduced at your own school?
4 Discuss the story as a group, and write a full account of the events from one point of view. Each group should choose a different character. Then each group in turn should answer questions from the class designed to create a full picture of what happened.
5 Have you ever in any way been involved in a similar situation?

* * *

The lie detector

Philip Agee had to take a lie-detector test when he applied to join the American espionage organisation, the CIA. At his preliminary interview he told some 'half-truths'. It remained to be seen whether the detector would spot these:

> Now we were ready for the test. The polygraph consists of three apparatuses which are attached to the body of the person being interrogated and which connect by tubes or cords to the desk ensemble. Each apparatus measures physiological changes, marked on moving graph paper by three pens. There are, accordingly, a blood pressure cuff that can be attached either to the arm or leg, a corrugated rubber tube about two inches in diameter that is placed snugly around the chest and fastened in the back, and a hand-held device with electrodes that is secured against the palm by springs that stretch across the back of the hand. The cuff measures changes in pulse and blood pressure, the test-tube measures changes in breathing rhythm, and the hand instrument measures changes in perspiration. I was hooked into the machine, told to look straight ahead at the wall, to be very still, and to answer only yes or no to each question. The interrogator was behind me at the desk ensemble facing the back of my head, and I answered to the wall in front.
>
> During the pre-test interview I had given my interrogator several half-truths, partly because I simply resisted his invasion of my life, and partly because I was curious about the effectiveness of the machine. Foolish child! As the cuff inflated I was conscious of increased pulse and my hands began to sweat profusely. Anticipating the questions that I should react on, I started to count the holes in the tiles in order to distract myself from the test. The interrogator passed very slowly from one question to another, pausing between each question. I answered yes or no and at the end he slipped in an unannounced question: had I answered all the questions truthfully? Dirty trick. I said 'yes', and after a few seconds the cuff deflated.
>
> I heard a shuffling of paper and he reviewed the chart as I remained still. He told me I could move a little but that if I was not particularly uncomfortable he would like me to remain seated and hooked up. Fine. He stayed behind the desk behind my chair, and started asking me what I was thinking about.... I would stick to my half-truths. They weren't lies anyway, and besides, I have heard that you can beat the machine if you stay consistent....
>
> The interrogator said we would go through the questions again, and that I hadn't done too well on the first two runs, adding that there is no way for me to be hired without successfully passing the test. Was

there anything I wanted to say or clarify? No. I was being truthful and maybe something was wrong with the machine.

From *Inside the Company* by Philip Agee, Penguin 1975

For discussion
1 What possibly happened next?
2 Philip Agee was eventually admitted to the CIA. Was the session with the lie detector a good way of deciding if he was eligible to join the Agency?
3 Have you ever been in a similar situation? — ie. where you have been examined very closely to determine whether you are telling the truth? Improvise the incident, or devise one.
4 The lie detector in this incident, measured changes in the subject's breathing, perspiration, etc. How do we usually determine if people are lying?
5 Important events can follow (and be caused by) the telling of a lie. (Troy, for example, fell because everybody believed a liar!) Can you think of any other historical incidents in which a lie had major consequences?
6 Think of an incident from your own life. Think of a way of telling it such that it *could* be true but perhaps is not. Alternatively, think of an entirely fictitious incident/story which also could be true ot untrue. Now tell each other your stories, and see how well other people can decide if they are *true or false*.

12 Aggression

aggress attack first, begin a quarrel.
aggression unprovoked attack; impulse to show hostility.
aggressive disposed to attack others, threatening; eager to quarrel; taking the offensive.
aggressor one who makes the first attack, especially if unprovoked; State that declares war on or first attacks another.

In some way or other, we are all of us aggresive, and equally, we are all the victims of one another's aggressivness. Take the following news story:

Boy plays truant from bullies
Mrs Alice Bowen has told school authorities she will keep her son Simon at home until the bullies who terrorise him have been disciplined by their headmaster.
Simon, aged 13, is so scared of the bullies — a group of older and bigger boys — that he played truant for a whole week until his mother discovered what was happening. Now, she says, Simon is too sick and nervous to go back to school.
'The bully boys were running what they called a protection racket, and other boys have to pay them money or they get beaten up. Simon couldn't afford to pay, and didn't want to.'
The education authority has told Mrs Bowen that the school is looking into the matter. 'In the meantime it is her legal duty to send her son back to school,' they added.

For discussion
1 Is this an unusual story in any way?
2 Bullies come in different shapes and sizes. Describe some of the ways in which you have ever been bullied, or have ever bullied others.
3 Will there always be bullies? If so, why do you think this is so?
4 How if at all, would you punish the bullies in this case?
5 Can you see any virtues in bullying? Is it in any way useful?
6 What are the different means we adopt to save ourselves from bullies? Devise and improvise a story to illustrate this.

* * *

Ritualised fights

Animals, of course, have as much capacity for aggression as humans have. And like humans, they engage in aggressive activities in which they follow certain rules about how far they can go: they keep to the rules, much as sportsmen do when playing a game. In the extract below, *Konrad Lorenz* gives two examples of such behaviour, one involving fish, the other involving deer:

> An impressive example of behaviour analogous to human morality can be seen in the ritualised fighting of many vertebrates. Its whole organisation aims at fulfilling the most important function of the rival fight, namely to acertain which partner is stronger without hurting the weaker. Since all human sport has a similar aim, ritualised fights give the impression of 'chivalry' or 'sporting fairness'. To this quality a cichlid species owes its American nickname. It is called 'Jack Dempsey', after the world champion boxer renowned for the fairness of his fighting. . . .
>
> For example, when two Jack Dempseys have opposed each other long enough with broadside threatening and tail-beating, one of them may be inclined to go on to mouth-pulling a few seconds before the other one. He now turns from the broadside position and thrusts with open jaw at his rival who, however, continues his broadsides threatening, so that his unprotected flank is presented to the teeth of his enemy. But the aggressor never takes advantage of this; he always stops his thrust before his teeth have touched the skin of his adversary.
>
> My friend the late Horst Siewert described and filmed an analagous process among fallow deer. In these animals, the highly ritualised antler fight, in which the crowns are swung into collision, locked together, and then swung to and fro in a special manner, is preceded by a broadside display in which both animals goose-step beside each other, at the same time nodding their heads to make the great antlers wave up and down. Suddenly, as if in obedience to an order, both stand still, swing at right-angles towards each other and lower their heads so that their antlers collide with a crash and entangle near the ground. A harmless wrestling match follows in which, just as in the mouth fights of the 'Jack Dempseys', the victor is the one who can hold out the longest. Among fallow deer too, one of the fighters sometimes wants to proceed, in advance of the other, to the second stage of the fight, and thus finds his weapon aimed at the unprotected flank of his rival — a highly alarming spectacle considering the heavy thrust of the heavy, jagged antlers. But more quickly even than the circhlid, the deer stops the movement, raises his head, and now, seeing

that his unwitting, still goose-stepping enemy is already several yards ahead, breaks into a trot till he has caught up with him and walks calmly, antlers nodding, in goose-step beside him, till the next thrust of the antlers leads, in better synchronisation, to the ring fight.

From *On Aggression* by Konrad Lorenz, Methuen, University Paperback 1967

For discussion

1 What do we mean by 'ritual' and 'ritualised'? Give examples of ritual in your daily life, at home and at school.
2 Do you agree with Lorenz that sports are 'ritualised fights'?
3 Think of any fight you have seen or taken part in. What kinds of rituals, if any, were observed?
4 The ritual fights among animals, observed by Lorenz, appear to have as their aim, the identifying of the stronger 'without hurting the weaker'. What, then, is the possible gain to the stronger?
5 What is the possible gain to the victor in any of the fights you have seen or taken part in?
6 Children usually are told off or punished for fighting. As a general rule, would you encourage or discourage them from fighting?
7 Devise an improvisation in which people fight with each other, but never actually come face to face.

* * *

Why do children behave aggressively? why do they grow up into aggressive adults? One view is that television is greatly to blame:

Violence on TV exhausts children
People in Britain, especially children, are being exposed to too much stimulus and excitement. As a result they are becoming mentally exhausted and need even stronger stimuli to be excited. This is the view of Professor Ivor Mills, of the department of medicine at Cambridge University.

Professor Mills is concerned at the hormonal effects of constant exposure to high levels of excitement, induced by violence in films and television.

'If you go on stimulating people like mad, it is not surprising that when a child goes to school next day he or she finds it boring', he said. 'A lot of people in our society have been stimulated to the point where if something frustrates them they are likely to be either verbally or physically aggressive.'

For discussion
1 Would you agree with Professor Mills?
2 Can you think of a specific instance when violence on TV has influenced you to behave violently?
3 Do you think TV may have a bad influence on others, even it it does not have a bad influence on you? Can you give an example to illustrate this?
4 Is there a great deal of violence on TV and in films? If you think there is, why do you think this is so? Can you see any dangers in eliminating it altogether? Is it possible to do so?
5 Devise a speech appealing for more violence on TV, or for its complete elimination. Consider all the various types of arguments and illustrations you might employ.

* * *

A national newspaper recently did a survey of young people's attitudes to fighting. They discovered that girls enjoyed fighting as much as boys do:

> *I will take on boys, too*
> Annie Maxwell, 14, from Chiswick, London, has been fighting ever since she can remember. She says, 'I don't know anyone who doesn't fight at some time. I never walk away from a fight. And it's not just girls. I'll fight with boys as well.'
> Annie, a 5 ft 8 in. amazon says: 'The toughtest fight I had was when I was 12. It was like a prizefight. We met outside school and there were crowds of spectators. I just had to win, and I did. I was cut and battered but the other girl gave up first. Then it was great. I was the centre of attraction.'

Interview each other in your groups, and write a feature story based on the interviews. Take the theme FIGHTING.

* * *

For improvisation

A teacher is marking some exercise books in the classroom, late one afternoon. All the pupils have gone home. Through the open window scuffling noises can be heard, followed by the dialogue below. From the window he can see nothing, and so the two fighters must be just round

Aggression

the corner, out of sight. This is what he hears:

Voice 1	Come here you!
Voice 2	No. No.
Voice 1	I said, come here.
Voice 2	No. Let me go.
Voice 1	(Threateningly) I'll kill you.
Voice 2	Ah.... (Tearfully) No.... Help!
Voice 1	Ah shut up! There's no one to hear you, so shut up.... (Brutally) There! (Sound of thumping)
Voice 2	Help! Ah! Ooh!
Voice 1	You've had this coming to you.
Voice 2	No.
Voice 1	Yes you have!
Voice 2	Aah. You bully! You great – ooh!
Voice 1	(Change of tone) Just a minute. Where's my wallet? What have you done with my wallet? You've pinched my wallet.
Voice 2	Stop mucking about. (Very relaxed)
Voice 1	It's you who's mucking about. Where's my wallet?
Voice 2	(In pain again) Aah! Ooh!
Voice 1	You heard me.
Voice 2	Help! Help! Help!

At this point, the teacher charges out of the room, into the corridor, down the stairs, out of the building, and round the corner. He discovers two boys (or two girls). One of them is in a state of collapse, and appears to be either laughing or crying or both. The other is blindly crawling around, looking for his or her glasses, which lie broken on the ground.

Discuss some of the possibilities to explain what is happening, and what might happen next. Then improvise the scene, from the point where the teacher arrives.

13 Fame and Fortune

Compare these three news stories:

1   *Arsenal snaps up young Brennan*
Arsenal have signed former England schoolboy skipper, Donald Brennan, as an apprentice professional.
Sixteen-year-old Brennan, who left school this week, told reporters he had been hoping and praying for the opportunity to come his way: 'I am absolutely overjoyed about this chance. All I want to do now is to get into the first team.'
A spokesman for Arsenal, said: 'We're pleased to sign the lad. Now we'll have to see what we can do with him.'

2   *Former champion dies in poverty*
One-time lightweight boxing champion Randolph Turpin died yesterday — 'lonely, out of work, and out of friends,' according to a neighbour who saw him shortly before he died. Seven years ago, Turpin reached fame and fortune as one of the leading lightweight boxers in the country. It was a hard, uphill struggle for the boy who always said he was from 'the wrong side of the street.'
But it was even harder for him at the top. He spent his money, drank too much, and soon disappeared from the big time. Promoters said he put on too much weight and was seldom sober.
In later years Turpin tried to make a new career — in all-in wrestling. But it did not work out as he hoped. And the boy who had been 'the brightest hope for British boxing' showed no great skill in the wrestling ring.
Those who remember him at the peak of his form will mourn the loss of a fine talent, and the waste of what should have been a great career.

3   *Punk Rock stars on the dole*
'We're on the dole, waiting for fame and fortune,' said local punk rock star, Jim Horner, today. 'The big offers are just around the corner, and we've just got to wait for them.'
Jim is, of course, the leader of The Skunks, the local group who have already made appearances up and down the country, and have twice featured on TV.
'It's no use being out at the factory when the phone calls come through from the record companies. So we're waiting at home, living off the dole. It's not bad. It's enough to live on, more or less,' said Jim.

Fame and Fortune

Asked what they would do if the big offers never come, Jim replied: 'They must do. If you can't be rich and famous, what's the point of doing anything?'

Jim is 16, and the youngest of the group. He liked school and says he did very well there. 'They were sorry to see me go,' he said. 'They were all begging me to stay on for the sixth form.'

For discussion

1 All three stories are in one way or another about 'success'. We all see 'success' in rather different ways. How do the people in these news stories see success? What does it mean to them?
2 What does success mean to us? What sacrifices are we prepared to make to achieve it?
3 All three stories leave a great deal unsaid. Choose one, and invent a fuller narrative. Perhaps extend the story forward and backward in time. You might like to choose one way of telling the story, such as a series of entries in the character's diary, or his letters to a friend, or perhaps a series of news stories marking the different stages of his career.
4 Stars and champions attract a vast public. They become idols. Why do we 'idolise' such people?
5 We all have success of one kind or another. We all have ambition of one kind or another. Think of an incident in your own life when you have been either within reach of great success, or have had success taken away from you. Tell us about it.
6 Choose one small incident related to any one of the three news stories and improvise it. (You might take, for instance, the rock star being invited to stay on for the sixth form, or the young footballer telling his family about the offer to turn professional.) Or choose an imaginary (or real) incident that in any way parallels these stories.

Structured improvisation

For three characters, mother (Ellen), father (Alec) and son (Ken).

Instructions for ALL THREE CHARACTERS: Father works in local government. Mother is a nurse. Ken is 14, and is doing well at school. It's very possible that he will eventually go on to university. He's especially good at languages. But he's a good all-rounder, with quite some talent for sports of all kinds, including boxing and football, and also for acting. Mother and father discourage Ken from spending too much time on these 'hobbies', and encourage him to do his homework and to prove his worth in the forthcoming GCE exams. Ken has many friends, including a girl-friend Alice, whose brother Jack is well-known locally as a schoolboy boxing champion. Mother and father like Alice very much: she's a nice, smart girl. *The scene takes place* at home. It is after supper, and Ken is doing some

homework. Father is reading the paper, and mother is doing the washing-up.
Instructions for KEN *(alone):* you are still doing well at school, but you have recently become especially interested in boxing. This is through your connection with Alice's brother, Jack, the schoolboy boxing champion. He took you along a couple of times to the gymnasium where he trains, and you started sparring with him — just for the fun of it. As it happened, Jack was impressed by you, and so was his trainer, and so for the last couple of months you have been going along, unbeknown to your parents, for special training sessions. You're told that you're really very promising, and Jack's trainer has decided to put you in for a schoolboys' tournament in four weeks' time. If you do well in this, there is every possibility of your being entered for some championship matches. Indeed the trainer (Mr Tony Philpots) tells you that you could very easily become a champion. You might even turn professional, he says. In fact, you have no wish to become a professional boxer, you would rather go on to university and study languages there. But you wish very much to take part in the tournament and go as far with the boxing (as an amateur) as you are able. But you have not yet raised the matter with your parents. They know nothing of it. You intend to speak to them this evening.
Instructions for ELLEN *(mother) alone:* you have been speaking to friends at work about your son and his cleverness at school, and especially about his cleverness with languages. They have told you that there will not be very much of a career in languages. There is too much competition for too few jobs. He would do better to devote his attention to maths and science, and become an engineer or technologist of some kind. You don't understand much about such things, but you're keen for Ken to do the right things. You will discuss the matter with him this evening, and also see what his father thinks.
Instructions for ALEC *(father) alone:* you met Alice's father in town today, during the lunch-break. In the course of the discussion, he told you something very alarming: Ken is taking up boxing. Alice's brother Jack took him along to his gymnasium, and some fool of a trainer there has told your Ken that he could end up a boxing champion. Apparently, Ken is entirely sold on the idea, and is thinking of giving up all ideas of going to university in order to give his attentions to boxing. As a start, he plans to take part in some tournament or other. You knew nothing about this, and are determined that nothing should come of such foolishness. You have a particular dread of boxing, because a friend of yours years ago, at school, was killed in an accident in the boxing ring. Not only that, but Ken *must* keep up the good work at school and go on to university. You will have absolutely none of this departure from the agreed plan. Ken has not yet spoken to you about it. But he's a good lad at heart, and you know he will be speaking to you soon enough. If he does not, then you will have to raise the matter yourself.

14 Evidence

Our knowledge of what happens in the world, past and present, is based on various kinds of evidence. Sometimes the evidence is so clearcut that there is no disputing it; as in the following case:

Rewards for children who chased man
Three schoolchildren who helped to arrest an armed man were each given cash rewards at Manchester Crown Court today.

The story of how they acted when Frederick Hayward, an unemployed electrician, fled empty-handed from a post office near their home was told to Judge Sir William Morris.

The judge said: 'The behaviour of these children really excites my admiration. They have shown great courage, resource and initiative.'

He said that £20 should go to Brian Wright, aged 14, and £10 each to Lynda Reid, aged 13 and her brother Robert, aged 11.

Earlier Mr Hayward, aged 23, had been jailed for two years. He had pleaded guilty to assaulting Mrs Margaret Wilson, a postmistress, with intent to rob.

Mr Jonathan Geake, for the prosecution, said that on July 26 Mr Hayward pushed his way past Mrs Wilson as she was closing for lunch. He held a knife at her side, and demanded money. But Mr John Wilson, her husband, set off the alarm, and Mr Hayward ran from the shop.

He was chased by Brian Wright and Lynda Reid, who were on bicycles. Mr Hayward threatened them, saying: 'Get away. If you come near me, I'll give it to you.'

Counsel said Lynda Reid gave up the chase but handed her bicycle to her brother, who helped Brian Wright to carry on the chase. Brian Wright eventually drew alongside Mr Hayward and grabbed his arm. Mr Hayward took out his knife just as police arrived, having been guided to the scene by Lynda Reid.

For discussion

1 Have you ever been in a situation like this? Have you ever given chase? or been chased?
2 How might the prisoner tell the story of what happened?
3 The Judge was very pleased with the children. They caught the criminal. Is it possible they could have caught the wrong man?

evidence was on one side, but the truth, as it happened, was on the other?

Now look at the next case:

Mistaken Identity

In 1976 Peter Hain was tried at the Old Baily with theft from a bank:

> 'On 24 October (1974), just before 1 pm, the man alleged to be Peter Hain went to Barclays Bank and asked for cash for change of a £10 note. The cashier, Mrs Lucy Haines, took out a bundle of £5 notes, intending to give the man two £5 notes in exchange. While she was getting the change ready the man grabbed the roll of notes and ran. The man was chased by an accountant from the Bank and by three boys. He dropped the money and escaped, but was recognised by the three boys afterwards when he was getting out of a car at W H Smith's. Peter Hain was later arrested and identified by the cashier from whom the notes had been stolen.'

The man in W H Smith's was Peter Hain. But he denied that he was also the man who stole the money from the Bank. No money was found, and no motive was given for the accused stealing the money. In effect, if the boys had not seen Hain later in W H Smith's and told the police that this was the bank thief, Hain would never have been suspected of or accused of the crime. Friends of the family were prepared to testify that Hain had been nowhere near the Bank at the time of the robbery. The prosecution case depended on the identification of Hain as the robber — by the boys, and also by the cashier. All four boys gave evidence. Three of them spoke as prosecution witnesses, one of them appeared for the defence.

The first to appear was Damian, 12 years old.

PROSECUTOR	When the man being chased turned into Oxford Road did you get an opportunity of seeing what he looked like?
DAMIAN	Yes.
PROS	When was that?
DAMIAN	He turned round to see where the second man was before he dropped the money. I saw his face. I also saw his face when I turned round to see what was happening in the High Street.
PROS	Tell us about the man's clothing.
DAMIAN	Blue check shirt, dark blue coloured jeans, brown Hush Puppy shoes, dark-rimmed glasses.
PROS	When you turned left into Oxford Road did you see any sign of the man you'd been chasing?

Mistaken Identity

DAMIAN	No. . . . We had nearly got to the church when we heard a car coming down the road behind us at nearly 60 miles an hour. We turned because we heard it coming down fast. It was a blue Volkswagen.
PROS	What did it do?
DAMIAN	Pulled up just in front of us and the driver ran into the side entrance of W H Smith's. . . . I thought I recognised the man as the man we had been chasing.
PROF	Did you recognise him by his clothes?
DAMIAN	His jeans and shirt were the same. So we followed him into Smith's, saw him buy some things and followed him out of the front entrance back to his car. . . . (He) drove off into the High Street and I went with John and Neil to have lunch at the Kentucky fried chicken place and then to the police station.
PROS	How long were you in the Kentucky?
DAMIAN	Ten minutes.
PROS	What had happened to Terry?
DAMIAN	He'd gone off to school.
PROS	You made a statement to the police on the same day. Did you omit to mention the presence of a fourth boy?
DAMIAN	Yes. Terry told us to keep him out of it.

Damian was later cross-examined by the defence counsel:

DEFENCE	Are you colour blind? (Pause. . .) Are you colour blind?
DAMIAN	No.
DEF	So you know the difference between blue and brown?
DAMIAN	Yes.
DEF	When the events were taking place, it was daylight?
DAMIAN	Yes.
DEF	You said the shirt was white with blue checks?
DAMIAN	Yes.
DEF	Others whom the thief actually passed have said the shirt he was wearing was white, cream or off-white. Was that correct? (No answer. The question is repeated.)
DAMIAN	No, Sir. . . .
DEF	When you were sitting outside this court yesterday, you were talking with John Brewster and Neil Lovelock, about the evidence you were going to give in this case, weren't you?

DAMIAN	No.
DEF	I'll repeat the question. Were the three of you together outside this court?
DAMIAN	Yes.
DEF	Were you talking about the case?
DAMIAN	(Pause. . .) Yes.

By the end of the three boys' evidence it was clear that they were confused about the truth, and had contradicted each other on most of the important issues. They could not even agree on where they had had lunch; Damian said in the Kentucky; Neil said in a sweetshop; John said in the baker's.

It was the evidence of the fourth boy, Terry MacLaren, that made a substantial difference to the case:

DEF	When you all walked back down Werter Road, did something happen near Smith's?
TERRY	We were outside, 25 yards from Smith's. A blue Volkswagen pulled up in front of us and a man got out and went into Smith's.
DEF	Did you see him?
TERRY	Yes.
DEF	What was your state of mind about the man?
TERRY	Well — it wasn't the thief — nothing like him.
DEF	What differences were there between the man from the Volkswagen and the man who had been chased?
TERRY	The man in Smith's had thick-rimmed glasses. His hair was shorter and neater. His shirt was rather the same but the design was different. He didn't have anything over his shirt and his jeans were darker than the first man's.
DEF	What about his height and build?
TERRY	About the same height. But the man from the Volkswagen was bigger, broader. He didn't have a long face like the first man. He had a roundish face. He was clean-shaven.
DEF	You saw the first man walking, and the man from the Volkswagen walking. Did you notice anything about the way either of them walked?
TERRY	The thief walked funny. It looked like he was knackered. His head was down. The man in Smith's walked normally. . . I said, 'That ain't the man.' Somebody said, 'Yes it is.' One said, 'We'll take the number to the police.' I said, 'You'll get an innocent

	man into trouble.' They said, 'We'll give it to the police. We'll get the afternoon off school and get a lift in a police car.' Then I said, 'I don't want to get involved if you're going to do that.' (Then) All four of us went into Coombes the bakers, bought cakes and ate them walking along. Then I went back to school and they went towards the police station.
DEF	Before you left the school that afternoon, did you see any of the other boys again?
TERRY	Yes — Damian and Neil. I said, 'What happened?' They said, 'The police told us they caught him on our evidence.' I nearly hit 'em. I was in a temper with them. On the way home, walking towards the swimming baths, they said, 'It was worth the afternoon off school.'

Hain was found not guilty by a majority verdict of the jury. Court evidence taken from Peter Hain's own account of the trial *Mistaken Identity*, Quaker Books 1976.

For discussion
1 The two boys give different accounts of the same experience. Judging from the extracts given here, which one, if either, do you find the more credible? Why?
2 Have you ever been in a position where your own evidence, given in good faith, was contradicted by an equally honest second witness? What happened?
3 Why is it that people can differ so sharply about what they see?
4 Peter Hain was accused of a serious crime for which there was no evidence against him except the identification of a small group of witnesses. There was no evidence of his having the money, nor was he caught at the scene of the crime. Do you think it is right to prosecute a man in such a case?
5 Have you ever yourself been seriously accused of something for which no evidence exists except identification? (ie. someone says they saw you do it.) What happened?
7 The witness Terry MacLaren was obviously of great importance to the defence. He recieved anonymous phone calls before the trial, threatening him, and warning him not to appear as a witness. During the trial and afterwards, he recieved more phone calls, similarly abusive, as well as anonymous letters. Why do you think this was?
7 Have you ever yourself been in a similar situation to Terry MacLaren? — subjected to various pressures designed to stop you telling the truth?

What did you do?
8 Have you ever tried to stop anyone else from teling the truth in such a situation? What happened?
9 It is a fairly dramatic and frightening experience to give evidence in a law court, and no doubt very different from giving the same evidence in an informal fashion. Think of something quite important that has happened to you in the past. (Perhaps an interview with the headmaster, for example.) Tell your group about it. Now stand before the class as a whole, and answer questions on it from two different people, *one of them* seeking to build up the story of what happened from your point of view and in great detail, and the other seeking to go over everything you have said to see if you contradict yourself or show gaps in your memory.

* * *

Structured improvisation

For three characters: a schoolgirl, a teacher and a headmistress.

Instructions for ALL THREE CHARACTERS: the teacher (Mr Riggs) had some trouble with the girl (Carol Burdett) during the last lesson on Friday afternoon, a History lesson. The girl kept on looking at her watch, the teacher got angry and took the watch from her. He also kept her in after school, after the rest of the class was dismissed. On the Monday morning after this, Mr Riggs is summoned to the Head's study. As he goes in he notices Carol Burdett sitting in the waiting room outside, crying.

Instructions for THE HEAD *(alone):* this morning you received a letter from Mr Burdett, complaining that the teacher had not only confiscated the watch during the lesson, but had also failed to return it. It is an extremely valuable gold watch (it cost £200 according to Mr Burdett) and he demands that it be returned forthwith. You decide to have a word with Riggs: he's a good teacher and you don't doubt that he will have a good explanation. But you are a little worried because you have found him slightly forgetful in the past, he is inclined to lose his class register, for example. As far as you can tell, Carol Burdett is normally well behaved. You will talk with Riggs alone, and then bring in Burdett and hand the watch back to her. Since she was rude to the teacher in class, you will no doubt (discreetly) reprimand her for this.

Instructions for MR RIGGS - *(alone):* you are confused to see Carol Burdett outside the Head's study, and crying. Could this be something to do with the trouble she caused you in class on Friday afternoon? You did nothing too terrible, did you? You didn't strike her. (You wouldn't dream of striking anyone.) You didn't swear at her. (You never swear at anyone.) You didn't say anthing too terribly unkind. (You do sometimes say very sharp and cutting things when your temper is roused.) You didn't drop her wretched watch. At least you don't think you did. You just gave it back to her. You remember it well. You had dismissed the rest of the class. Then you gave her the watch. Yes. You're sure of that. Your memory does let you down sometimes, but you remember that. (You forgot to hand in the class dinner money a month ago. That caused a lot of trouble. And quite a few jokes. It was the dinner money, wasn't it? — or was it the list of marks for the second year history exam?) It's not that your memory is going — besides, you're still a young man. It's just that you do have a lot of things to remember.

Instructions for **CAROL** *(alone);* you had reached home on Friday before you realised that you did not have the watch. But on the way home, you stopped in the park to chat with friends, and then called into some shops, met some more friends, and so it was two hours after leaving school before you actually got into the house. Immediately you realised that your expensive gold watch, a family heirloom passed on from your great-grandmother, and allegedly worth £200, was missing. You cannot really remember whether or not Mr Riggs gave it to you. It's just possible that he did. But you cannot remember it. It's possible that he did, and that you lost it on the way home. (It is a small wrist watch.) But you dared not tell your father that you might have lost it, and you did honestly expect it to be still with Mr Riggs. After all, it's not the kind of thing you lose. So you told father that Mr Riggs forgot to give it back to you and that you were too afraid to ask for it. You are now very upset, becuase you know that father has written an angry letter to the Headmistress. No doubt Mr Riggs *does* have the watch and will hand it over to you, but if he does not, you will have no alternative but to stick absolutely to the story as you told it to your father.

The scene begins as Riggs knocks on the door of the Head's study. Burdett waits outside until she is called.

15 School

At the time of giving the talk below, Keith was a 15-year-old student preparing to take the CSE exam in English. Part of this exam involves each student in giving a short talk to a small group of other students. Keith's group went through a trial run, and everyone spoke to the others about such subjects as hobbies, controversial issues, etc. Keith took as his theme *Parents and Teachers*. He talked very expressively and spontaneously about the kinds of pressures exerted on him by both parents and teachers, and the way he felt rejected by parents, because they wanted him to be someone he wasn't, and by most teachers, because they had decided he was no good. This is an extract from his talk:

> That's the trouble with some teachers. If — if you do something wrong in one subject, then they — and it's not their subject, then they think, oh well, he done bad in that subject — so — I'll say that he's doing bad in mine, before they've even listened to you. That's what happens to me. I'm not feeling sorry for meself or that, but, you know, if I did try, and then I don't think I could do any good, because a lot of teachers just listen to the staff-room chat, and they go by that. They've heard what I am. Because, before I come to school, my brothers was here, and they wasn't all that good. They used to muck about. And I was accepted as bad, when I came, although I am, but if I wasn't — if I intended to really try, I think — you know, I don't think I would have been able to get on, because some teachers just wouldn't have accepted it, that I was going to try, because my brothers were there and so — they wouldn't accept it that I would. And — this is the trouble with a lot of teachers, and not that — um — I'm not all that bright or I muck about quite a lot, they just — they just got the same against me, they, you know, even if I try now. . . .
> The other day I said to the teacher, 'Um, Sir, when will we be going to Norway, because I'm interested in it.' So he said, 'Well, we've been picking it out of an hat, because there's so many who want to go. I'm sure your name will come out.' But he meant 'I don't want you to go really.' And I'm sure if they picked it out of an hat my name would come out, cos I don't think they do it fairly anyway, and so that's what I reckon would happen to me, and some boys who haven't done anything wrong. They — they just get accepted as something

different to what they are. If they've done one thing bad, then everything's supposed to be bad to them.
But some teachers are all right. They accept you. . . .

Keith goes on to describe an incident where he is called out of class to see another teacher. When he comes back to the classroom —

> The teacher said, 'I see that's all you are, a scholar of English'. He thought I got the cane or something, and so — he — cos he wanted me to get the cane off this teacher. He wanted me to have done something bad cos he — that's the only subject I try in and he knows it, and so when — when I told him, 'No you're wrong sir,' he just went all red and was right choked, and said, 'Don't be insolent.' And that's what most of the teachers do to me, because I'm marked I suppose, and that's what happens to a lot of boys.
>
> From *Understanding Children Talking*, by Nancy Martin and others, Penguin Education 1976

For discussion

1 Do you find yourself in sympathy with any of the points made by Keith in his talk?
2 How much do you learn about Keith from his talk?
3 He mentions a variety of small incidents that have occurred at school. Can you fill out the details of any one of them, to make a fuller story of what might have happened?
4 Have any similar incidents ever happened to you? Improvise them.
5 Make a rough plan for a talk on the same theme, *Parents and Teachers*, and give the talk to the other members of your group. After the talk, have a small discussion about it. How far do new points emerge from the discussion? In what ways does discussion add to the points made in the talk?
6 Find an extract from literature (or the press) that illustrates the same theme. Read the extracts to the other members of your group. Choose one to read to the whole class.
7 Devise a 'documentary' entitled, *Parents and Children*. Work out a way of presenting it in sections, each with its own heading — such as 'Starting School', 'Winning Prizes', 'Truants' and so on. Each group might now choose one of the headings and work out ways of documenting and dramatising them. The final programme might include (i) improvisations (ii) readings from literature (iii) talks (iv) accompanying leaflet/booklet (v) wall display of photographs, written work, newsclips etc and (iv) tape recordings, perhaps of interviews with 'outsiders' such as parents, students in other classes, or other teachers.

16 Orders are Orders

All of us, most of the time, have to do (and do) what is expected of us and what we are told. We have, in all sorts of ways, to obey orders. Law, civilisation, morality and convention all rest on people's basic willingness to conform, to obey. But this also presents problems. The first example is a fairly extreme but not untypical illustration:

The Face of the Third Reich

Rudolf Hoss was the commandant of the concentration and extermination camp at Auschwitz. He talked of his childhood and youth:

> I had been brought up by my parents to be respectful and obedient towards all grown-up people, and especially the elderly, regardless of their social status. I was taught that my highest duty was to help those in need. It was constantly impressed upon me in forceful terms that I must obey promptly the wishes and commands of my parents, teachers, priests, etc., and indeed of all grownup people, including servants, and that nothing must distract me from this duty. Whatever they said was always right.
> These basic principles on which I was brought up became part of my flesh and blood. I can still clearly remember how my father, who, on account of his fervent Catholicism, was a determined opponent of Hitler's Government and its policy, never ceased to remind his friends that, however strong one's opposition might be, the laws and decrees of the State had to be obeyed unconditionally.
> From my earliest youth I was brought up with a strong awareness of duty. In my parents' house it was insisted that every task be exactly and conscientiously carried out. Each member of the family had his own special duties to perform.

And of his role as mass murderer for the Nazis:

> I had nothing to say. I could only say Jawohl! We could only execute orders without thinking about it. From our entire training the thought of refusing an order just didn't enter one's head, regardless of what kind of order it was.

And:

> I am completely normal. Even while I was carrying out the task of extermination I led a normal family life and so on. Let the public continue to regard me as the bloodthirsty beast, the cruel sadist and the mass murderer; for the masses could never imagine the commandant of Auschwitz in any other light. They could never understand that he, too, had a heart and that he was not evil.

Hess was tried before the Polish Supreme People's Court as a war criminal, and was condemned to death. He was hanged at Auschwitz in 1947. This extract from his self-portrait is taken from *The Face of the Third Reich*, by Joachim C Fest, Weidenfeld and Nicolson 1970

For discussion
1. Hoss's account of his childhood focuses on one key aspect — learning to obey. Why does he focus it in this way?
2. What aspects of his childhood might he leave out? Why?
3. Hoss declares that he is normal, that he has a heart, that he leads a normal family life, and so on. Is this plausible? .... If you accept it as plausible, for the sake of argument, what does he actually mean by it?
4. In this extract, Hoss uses circumstances of his upbringing to explain why he behaved in certain ways as an adult. He tries to use his past life as a defence against the charges brought against him. Can you think of any instances where this might exempt someone, in your eyes, from responsibility for their actions?
5. Think of a situation, perhaps from real life, and perhaps from your own experience, where someone has done something which to your mind is unforgiveable and entirely wrong. Describe the incident. Now find ways of defending the person, and of explaining why he/she did it.
6. Think of a situation when you did as you were told, but knew that it was wrong to do it. Or think of a possible situation on the same lines. Tell the group about it. Improvise it.

* * *

The Last Secret
In 1945 some 50 000 Cossacks, men, women and children, many of them refugees from Stalin's Communism, found themselves prisoners of the Allies. They had ended up fighting for Hitler — indeed they had no alternative, since they would have been killed by Stalin. They believed that

Britain and the USA would understand their plight and would show mercy, but in fact Roosevelt and Churchill had already pledged to Stalin (at Yalta) that they would be returned to Russia. From 1945 to 1947 they were systematically and forcibly repatriated, many of them committing suicide rather than face Stalin's revenge.

A British officer responsible for some thousand Cossacks, later wrote:

> We looked after them for several weeks and we found them a very pleasant lot. They told us they were frightened of being sent back to Russia, but we said, 'Oh no, the British would never do such a thing.' Then we got this order that in three days they were all to be handed back. We were shattered. Our men kept coming to us and saying, 'Look, these Cossacks say they're going to be sent back and they'll all be shot.' But until we got the order we didn't believe it could happen. The feeling was that they'd be found somewhere to live. I'd never seen my blokes quite as shaken as they were over that particular incident. And they'd been with me for years. They were used to war. They'd come up all the way from Salerno. But they didn't like the idea of all these men being murdered in cold blood.

From *The Last Secret* by Nicholas Bethell, Deutsch 1974

For discussion

1 The officer eventually carried out the order, despite his feelings. What arguments might the Cossacks have used to dissuade him? Think of a roughly similar situation from your own experience, and improvise the arguments you used, or might have used.

2 The Cossacks' fate had been sealed at the Yalta agreement – unbeknown to them. Stalin wanted them back for his revenge, for they had fled from his domination and joined the Germans in the War, and Churchill and Roosevelt had more important matters to worry about (such as winning the war against Germany and Japan). They were a small pawn in a very big game. Can you think of any occasion in your own life when you have been 'a small pawn'? What happened?

3 Can you think of any occasion when you were 'the big power' and you treated someone else as 'the small pawn'? What happened?

4 Stalin wanted revenge on people who had refused to follow his lead (and specifically, who refused to fall under Russian domination). Have you ever been the victim of someone's revenge? Do you know anyone who has? What happened? Has any one ever been the victim of your revenge?

* * *

The Charge of the Light Brigade

Sometimes orders are ambiguous. When they are obeyed, even so, disasters can follow. The classic instance of this is the celebrated charge of the Light Brigade at the Battle of Balaclava, in the Crimean War. What happened was basically simple: a commander-in-chief, viewing the battlefield from the top of a hill, saw an excellent opportunity for the cavalry to attack the enemy (the Russians) and recover lost ground. He sent orders to that effect, to the general in charge of the cavalry. The general, unlike the commander, was on low ground, and his view was blocked by mounds and ridges. The order to attack did not specify in which direction, and the general chose a direction which was not illogical (he knew the enemy were there) but which proved to be the wrong one. It led him and the men straight into the enemy's artillery.

In this extract from Christopher Hibbert's account of the Charge, the principal characters are:
Lord Raglan, the Commander-in-Chief, who sends the order to
Lord Lucan, the Lieutenant-General,
Lord Cardigan, the Brigade-Commander (and Lucan's brother-in-law)
and *Captain Nolan,* the Aide-de-Camp.

> The order read: 'Lord Raglan wishes the cavalry to advance rapidly to the front — follow the enemy and try to prevent the enemy carrying away the guns. Troop Horse Artillery may accompany. French cavalry in on your left. Immediate.'
>
> Captain Nolan galloped up to Lord Lucan and handed him the order. Lucan read it slowly, with that infuriating care which drove more patient men than Nolan to scarcely controllable irritation. 'Lord Raglan's orders are that the cavalry should attack immediately,' said Captain Nolan, already mad with anger. 'Attack, sir! Attack what? What guns, Sir? Where and what to do?' 'There, my Lord!' Nolan flung out his arm in a gesture more of rage than of indignation. 'There is your enemy! There are your guns!'
> And leaving Lord Lucan as muddled as before, he trotted away.
>
> The trouble was that Lord Lucan had no idea what he was intended to do. He could not, on the plain, see nearly as far as Lord Raglan could on the hills above him. The only guns in sight were at the far end of the North Valley, where a mass of Russian cavalry was also stationed. These must presumably be the ones Lord Raglan meant. Certainly Nolan's impertinent and flamboyant gesture had seemed to point at them. His mind now made up, Lord Lucan trotted over to Cardigan and passed on the Commander-in-Chief's order. Coldly polite, Lord Cardigan dropped his sword in salute.

'Certainly, Sir,' he said, in his loud but husky voice. 'But allow me to point out to you that the Russians have a battery in the valley in our front, and batteries and riflemen on each flank.'
'I know it,' replied Lucan. 'But Lord Raglan will have it. We have no choice but to obey.'
'The Brigade will advance,' Lord Cardigan said in a strangely quiet voice.

For the first fifty yards the Light Brigade advanced at a steady trot. The guns were silent. Suddenly the beautiful precision and symmetry of the advancing line was broken. Inexcusably galloping in front of the commander came that 'impertinent devil' Nolan. He was waving his sword above his head and shouting for all he was worth. He turned round in his saddle and seemed to be trying to warn the infuriated Lord Cardigan and his first line of his men that they were going the wrong way. But no one heard what words he was shouting, for now the Russians had opened fire, and his voice was drowned by the boom and crash of their guns. A splinter from one of the first shells fired flew into Nolan's heart.

Cardigan and Lucan survived the massacre: Raglan asked Cardigan —

'What did you mean, Sir, by attacking a battery in front, contrary to all the usages of warfare and the customs of the service?'
'My Lord,' Cardigan said, confident of his blamelessness, 'I hope you will not blame me, for I received the order to attack from my superior officer, in front of the troops.'
It was, after all, a soldier's complete indemnification. Lord Cardigan rode back to his yacht with a clear conscience. To Lord Lucan, Lord Raglan said sadly, 'You have lost the Light Brigade.'
Lucan vehemently denied it, and he later wrote, 'I do not intend to bear the smallest particle of responsibility. I gave the order to charge, under what I considered a most imperious necessity, and I will not bear one particle of the blame.'

Of the 673 men who had charged down the valley less than 200 had returned. The Russians, as well as the allies, were deeply moved by such heroism. General Liprandi could not at first believe that the English cavalry had not all been drunk.

Adapted from *The Destruction of Lord Raglan* by Christopher Hibbert, Longmans 1961

For discussion
1 From the evidence as it appears in this extract, is any one to blame?
2 Find a copy of Tennyson's poem 'The Charge of the Light Brigade'.

In what ways does Tennyson's account differ from the above extract?
3 Lucan hesitated before carrying out the order, presumably because he was not sure he understood it. But he then persuaded himself that he did understand it, and carried it out. With hindsight, we can see that he should have carried on hesitating. Why didn't he? Why didn't he check the position before doing anything? (He was later criticised by Raglan for not doing so.)
4 Have you ever been in the position Lucan was in at the moment of hesitating? What did you do?
5 Choose any *one* of the leading characters from this incident, and build up a portrait/biographical sketch of the man. Do some research, perhaps looking at encyclopaedias, and at studies of the Crimean War, such as those by Christopher Hibbert (The Destruction of Lord Raglan) and by C Woodham-Smith (The Reason Why). There is also a 'Jackdaw' on the War, and this is well worth looking at.

Take the role of the character you've studied, and answer questions from the class, as if you are the man himself. The questions will range over your entire life.
6 Improvise any incidents from the Charge, and devise scenes from other parts of the characters' lives.

* * *

Structured improvisation

There are three characters, all of them university lecturers.
(NB This is devised for two girls and one boy, but the characters could be all girls, or all boys, or whatever is convenient in the particular class. The names given here should be dropped, and the players should keep their own names.)

Instructions for ALL THREE: you lecture in the History department at the University of Wessex. You are young, ambitious, and popular with your students. The students in the third and final year of the B.A. in History are all eligible for the Cranshaw Prize, which is awarded annually to the most outstanding student in your subject. The prize gives the winner a cash award of £1,500 plus the opportunity to do further study for a year at an American university, with all expenses paid. Although all 24 history students in their third year have on this occasion entered for the Prize, for which they have to write a long essay on the subject of their choice, the three of you have read all the essays and have eliminated all of them but six. The Professor (Wilkinson) who runs your department, has given you the shared job of choosing the winner. He wants your nomination today, and is expecting a call from you not later than half an hour hence. (He is about to fly off with his wife on a lecture tour of Australia, and wishes to announce the name of the winner before he goes.) The three of you have re-read the six finalists' essays, and now meet to decide the winner.

Instructions for MARY *(alone):* you cannot decide which of two of the essays should win the prize. The essay on the French Revolution by a student called Alice Grindle, whom you only vaguely know, is brilliant and incisive, but so is the very different essay by a favourite student of yours, John Cox, who has written very cleverly on the slave trade in America. You feel they should share the prize, if this is possible, but in fact the instructions are that it can only go to one candidate. This is a shame. But you do not like any of the other essays and you do like John Cox — a very talented and hard-working young man, well worth encourageing. In general, you see yourself as a co-operative person, and you are always pleased to be in the good books of Professor Wilkinson. Your prospects in the university world largely depend on his continuing favour.

Instructions for SONIA *(alone):* you are a very brilliant historian, far and away the most brilliant lecturer in your subject in this university. The other two, (Mary and Bernard) are way below you in professional standards, though they probably don't realise this. You are clear-headed, and say what you think and know what you are saying. There is no question that none of the candidates this year is worthy of the Cranshaw Prize. You intend to see to it that no Prize is awarded. The pity of it is that such poor work should be receiving any sign of encouragement, and when you eventually become a professor much higher standards will prevail. Of course, you must stay in the good books of Professor Wilkinson if you wish to progress up the ladder. But you imagine that he will be impressed by your insistence on high standards, and that it will be worth your while to make it clear that the refusal to award the Cranshaw prize was at your insistence. If the worst comes to the worst, and you have to give the prize to someone, then you would give it to Fay Timmings, who wrote a pedestrian and long-winded essay on Catherine the Great. But you would only nominate her with extreme reluctance. And the rest were absolute rubbish.

Instructions for BERNARD *(alone):* you are the most intelligent of the three, and so you are the one who is most likely to know a brilliant student when you see one. You consider the best student of the year (and perhaps of any year) to be Kay Standing, but as luck would have it, she has written an essay that is nowhere near the standard of which she is capable. So you will have to do a little careful manipulating of the other two judges in order to win the prize for her. Your technique will be to pretend to like another student's essay (Fay Timmings wrote one on Catherine the Great. It was awful, but you could pretend to be very impressed by it.) You will then let it be known that you met Mrs Wilkinson at a cocktail party last night. She was a little drunk, as usual, and unwittingly told you that Wilkinson has read the essays himself, and thinks Kay Standing's is far and away the best. You will tell this to the other two as if you don't know that you ought to, and as if you don't even know that it's significant. It's a lie, of course, though Mrs Wilkinson does tend to drink and talk too much. You know that both of the other judges will fall over backwards to please their boss, Professor Wilkinson, and that they will see his preference for Kay Standing as an absolute order for them to obey. If they don't, you will subtly apply pressure for them to do so.

The scene begins in Bernard's tutorial room. He is offering a glass of sherry to Sonia and Mary.

(NB Once the scene had got under way, arrange for a messenger to come in with a brief note from the Professor: 'Must have your decision promptly. No nonsense, and no dramas, please! — Wilkinson')

17 Red Tape

One of the many complexities of modern life is the abundance of rules and regulations, and of the people who enforce them. There are many depressing episodes in novels, films (and of course in real life!) of people held up, delayed, defeated even by red tape — by rules and regulations, sections and sub-sections, orders and details.

The three extracts quoted here, illustrate the prevalence of red tape in three quite different settings:

Parkinson's Law

Red tape increases as government increases its power; civil servants of various kinds are appointed to supervise and carry out the wishes of government; and the civil servants increase in number as the various regulations also increase. To a large extent, the increase in civil servants carrying out the rules laid down by the government, is independent of the power of the government itself. In other words, the government's power may *decrease* while the civil servants' labour force *increases*. C Northcote Parkinson has drawn attention to this and has even suggested that the number of civil servants are bound to increase as power declines — that this is a law, in fact.

He calls it *Parkinson's law:*

> Parkinson's Law was first published in Britain in 1958, the central theme of its key chapter suggesting that a Civil Service expands by an inexorable rule of growth, irrespective of the work, if any, which has to be done.
>
> Take the Admiralty, to begin with, as our first and classic example of administrative proliferation. . . . . In 1914, 4 336 officials could administer what was then the largest navy in the world. 1967 represents the point at which we have become practically powerless, by which period over 33 000 civil servants are barely sufficient to administer the navy we no longer possess.
>
> (And) the War Office need never shirk comparison with the Admiralty. In 1935 a civilian staff of 9 442 men sufficed to administer an Army

reduced to 203 361 officers and men. By 1966 a civilian staff of 48 032 was giving encouragement to some 187 000 men in uniform, a 7.9% reduction in fighting strength being accompanied by a 408% increase in paperwork.

Parkinson goes on to suggest that a further law can be detected in the workings of the civil service: *the law of delay*. In effect, not only will civil servants create delays whenever matters are placed before them, but as time goes on, the delays will inevitably become greater. He gives many illustrations of how this happens, and cites the case of the civil servant trying to get something done, and with this in mind, sending out a memorandum:

> But here lies one of the most dangerous traps in his path. In former times, and even it is rumoured, today, he would seek to give his ideas the widest circulation and have them printed or duplicated in large numbers. Because it was uneconomic in time and expense to set up the type or cut the stencil more than once, he always ordered spare copies. Where 78 people were to have copies he would order 100, just in case more would be needed; where 780, he would order 1 000. But the spare copies represented a waste, deplorable for any administrator. The natural reaction was to distribute them to those marginally interested in the issue. But each time even more copies were added, for distribution lists like many things have an innate principle of growth. And just as inevitably, the lengthening list extended to people who were decreasingly literate. More and more people at lower and lower levels were spending longer and longer time reading what concerned them less and less.

Adapted from *The Law of Delay* by C Northcote Parkinson, Murray 1970

For discussion
1 What kinds of red tape have you yourself come across?
2 Is red tape inevitable? Can things be organised without it?
3 Think of a situation in which you are delayed very seriously by red tape of some kind or another. Improvise it.

* * *

All organisations in some way or other require red tape — schools included. The following is an account of the way some schools reward good work and punish bad behaviour:

> The teaching master will fill in a *Pink Card* when a boy has done good

work for that boy's ability. He then sends it to the Head of Department who passes it on to the Headmaster, who passes it on to the Deputy Headmaster, who sends it to the Housemaster, who gives it to the boy to take home. After three or four of these, the Head asks to see the boy's exercise books and perhaps will give him a Headmaster's Commendation on printed decorated paper in assembly. The *White Card* is for consistently bad work. It goes through the same process but is not handed to the boy.

>From 'Teaching in Comprehensive Schools' a second report by
The Incorporated Association of Assistant Masters

For discussion

1 What do you think of the system outlined above? How does it compare with the system used in your own school?
2 Think of a situation in which the system of Pink and White Cards goes wrong. (What are some of the various ways in which this might happen?) Improvise the situation.

* * *

Chinese Red Tape

Imperial China was famous for its vast network of rules and regulations, the abundance of civil servants (the mandarins), and its complicated and rigid class system. Everyone belonged to one of ten grades. But there is evidence that in the modern Communist China set up by Mao Tse Tung, much of the old tradition lingers on:

> Old China's social system had only ten classes. We have progressed since then: the Maoist bureaucracy today has thirty classes. In all their contacts with foreigners, the Chinese civil servants insist on being given the exact title, function, and position of each person, so as to be able to gauge precisely the length of red carpet each should have: any uncertainty about this makes them uneasy to the point of anxiety. In fact they only want to apply to others the precise and rigid classifications that rule their own official life and give it such splendid orderliness. Nothing, no futile detail is left to chance: the place of an official photograph in the newspaper, its size, the presence or absence of important persons in it, the order in which the names of the leaders are given — all have meaning and are formally organised.

> In China, there are no cars but civil servants' cars: all civil servants (mandarins) travel in cars and only civil servants travel in cars. (Old people and people gravely ill and on their way to hospital, must do

with a wheelbarrow or cart pushed by friendly neighbours.) Since all cars are official cars, the simple fact of sitting in the back seat of a limousine is equivalent to a 'free pass'. If you have to do business in a government building and you come on foot, you are sure to be stopped by a sentry, or a doorkeeper, or an usher with whom you will have to discuss your visit at length before being allowed to pass through the first gate. If you come by car, on the other hand, the various watchdogs will swing the iron grill of the gate wide open as soon as they espy you from afar and you can zip through without even having to slow down.

In professional bureaucratic life, not to use a car sometimes seems as indecent as dressing only in underwear. To ride in a car marks you as an official, but the model, colour and size will vary according to your importance.

From an article by Simon Leys in 'The New York Review of Books',
June 1977, Ellsworth, New York

For discussion

1 Do all societies have 'classes'? Does our own? (What evidence do you have to support your answer?)
2 In Communist China, the car is a sign of rank or status, and it automatically confers certain privileges on its occupants. Can you think of any equivalent to this in your own country?
3 Can you think of any equivalent to this in your own school?
4 Think of a situation in which (like the Chinese mandarin trying to decide the class of the person he is talking to) two people are not sure how to 'place' each other, and so are not sure how they ought to treat each other. (List some of the possible settings in which such a problem might occur in your own lives — present or future.) Improvise the scene.

* * *

Structured improvisation

This is for two characters. A woman and a boy. The woman is the assistant to the Personnel Officer of an Insurance Company. The boy has recently left school and has written a letter of application in reply to an advertisement for a trainee insurance clerk. There are very few jobs of any kind on the market at this time, and there are probably many applications for this job. *The boy (GEORGE GREEN)* had a post card acknowledging his application; then he had a letter (printed) inviting him for an interview in three weeks' time; George arrived for the interview an hour and a half ago, at the time specified in the letter. He has been waiting in an outer office ever since. The office is filled, and re-filled, with youngsters like himself who are called into the inner office to meet the *assistant Personnel Officer, MRS SPALDING*. Each of them is interviewed for ten minutes exactly, and then leaves. Now it is George's turn.

The advertisement read:

> Trainee clerks required by Greater Security Insurance Company at their High Street Branch. Must have good school record and neat handwriting. Apply in writing, stating age and qualifications, to the Personnel Officer, Reference APO/67/RS (5), enclosing SAE and names of two referees.

George in his reply said that he is 16 years old, that he has a CSE in five subjects including English (Grade 2), that he played football for the school first eleven, and that his referees are his former House Master, and a businessman, a friend of his father's.

Instructions for MRS SPALDING *(alone):* the company were overwhelmed with applications for the clerical posts, and in fact the three vacancies have already been filled. But you are under strict instructions not to reveal this. Your company have decided that you will interview all the condidates in order that no one can say they were not given a fair chance. The company have their good name to consider and to look after. In fact, the posts were filled by young people who were moved over from an office in another town (one of the company's other branches) that had closed down. Your job as far as George Green is concerned is to ask him countless questions, designed to clarify what kind of career he had at school and what kind of person he is. You will also tell him about the job — the need to be trustworthy, to write neatly, to be patient and learn from those above him. You do not actually know very much about the job, but you have a broad impression of what a junior clerk does. There is a great deal of filing, for instance. You will be charming, courteous, and efficient. On no account must you give any one cause for complaint, for you might then lose your own job. You will give no indication whether or not George will get the job, though you of course know that there is no longer a job to get. You will simply point out that you will report back to the chief Personnel Officer, and he will confer with the branch manager, and he will make a recommendation to head office. And so all candidates will eventually hear from you. (And don't forget the time: ten minutes per candidate.)

Instructions for GEORGE GREEN *(alone):* you are desperate for a job.

You are depressed with being out of school and out of work. Your parents have urged you to make a good impression and you are determined to do so. While you are waiting you go over all the possible questions you might be asked, and also remind yourself of the need to be courteous, clear-spoken, and so on. You have a spotless school record, apart from a rather silly business two years ago when you started playing truant with a boy down the road. You were punished for this, got over such silliness, and have done well since. You hope that nothing of this will come out at the interview. You are not at all keen to be a clerk, but beggars can't be choosers. You'd rather emigrate to Canada and get work on a farm there, but your parents don't approve of this idea. So this will have to remain a secret ambition for the future. You desperately want this job.

18 Winning

The hero of John McGahern's novel *The Dark* has had a lonely, poor and unhappy childhood. But he's good at his school-work, and there is just a chance of winning a scholarship from his Roman Catholic school to university. His father, Mahoney, is as eager for the result as the boy himself:

> The exam result arrived the first week in August. Days of pestering the postman out on the road ended.
> 'Anything today?'
> The voice shook but tried laughably not to betray its obvious care, it was an unconcerned question.
> 'No. Nothing today,' he cycled past the gate, amusement in his voice, mixture of contempt and superiority of understanding, the green braid on his tunic.
> The day he produced the letter, there was no need to open it to know what it was, the postmark was plain. He just stared at it, the world reduced to its few square inches. He didn't notice the postman noisily mount his bike again and cycle off. The problem was how to open it, it shook violently in his hands. He tore it clumsily at last and he had to rest it against the gate, his hands were shaking so much, in order to read. HIs eyes clutched up and down at the words and marks as if to gulp it with the one look into the brain.
> It was only slowly it grew clear, the whole body trembling. He'd got the Scholarship, everything. He started to tremble, laughing, tears in the eyes, and then he rested against the gate, it couldn't be true. He read it again. . . . .
>
> 'You did it. There's marks for you. That's what'll show them who has the brains round here,' Mahoney shouted as he read.
> 'Congratulations,' he shook his head in the manner of a drama. 'Come and congratulate your brother.'
> They came and shook his hand and smiled up at him with round eyes, and that was the first cooling. They looked at him as different, and he knew he was the same person as before, he'd been given a lucky grace, he wanted it to be theirs as much as his, but he was changed in their eyes, they'd not accept he was the same.

'We'll go to town, the pair of us,' Mahoney was shouting. 'This is no day for work. A day like this won't arrive many times in our lives.' They dressed and went to town. Mahoney talked nonstop on the way. There was nothing to do but be silent and listen. The flood of generosity was choked. He was playing a part in Mahoney's joy, he was celebrating Mahoney's joy and not his own. He grew bored and restless but that was the way the day was going to go. Let it happen, let it happen, and let it be over as quickly as possible.

> From *The Dark* by John McGahern, Faber 1965
> Reprinted by permission of A D Peters and Co Ltd

For discussion

1 There is a sense of disappointment about the hero's 'winning'. Why is this? What does this tell us about him?
2 His father is very excited about the scholarship. What's likely to happen when they 'go to town'?
3 How might the father tell about the day's events — to friends, to relatives, to strangers even?
4 Have you ever been in a similar situation? What happened?
5 Devise a plot for improvisation, in which someone wins (or loses) something of great importance to him.

* * *

Gamesmanship — the art of winning games without actually cheating

Sometimes we win over our rivals by methods that are not strictly honourable even though they cannot be labelled strictly illegal. Stephen Potter describes various such methods in his studies of 'Gamesmanship, the art of winning games without actually cheating'. Here he talks about giving advice to your opponent in such a way as subtly to demoralise him:

> In my own view there is only one correct time when the gamesman can give advice: and that is when the gamesman has achieved a useful though not necessarily a winning lead. Say three up and nine to play at golf, or in billiards, sixty-five to his opponent's thirty. For example, in billiards:
> *Gamesman:* Look... may I say something?
> *Layman:* What?
> *Gamesman:* Take it easy.
> *Layman:* What do you mean?
> *Gamesman:* I mean — you know how to make the strokes, but you're

stretching yourself on the rack all the time. Look. Walk up to the ball. Look at the line. And make your stroke. Comfortable. Easy. It's as simple as that.

In other words, the advice must be vague, to make certain it is not helpful. But, in general, if properly managed, the mere giving of advice is sufficient to place the gamesman in a practically invincible position.

And here he examines the techniques of demoralising an opponent who is temporarily winning. These include subtle attempts to *break the flow* of your opponent's concentration:

> For example, at lawn tennis, opponent having won six consecutive points:
> *Gamesman:* (calling) Wait a minute.
> *Opponent:* What's wrong?
> *Gamesman:* Those damn kids!
> *Opponent:* Where?
> *Gamesman:* Walking across your line of sight.
> *Opponent:* What?
> *Gamesman:* I said, 'Walking across your line of sight.'
> *Opponent:* I can't see anyone.
> *Gamesman:* What?
> *Opponent:* I say I CAN'T SEE ANYONE.
> *Gamesman:* (continues less distinctly) . . . .bang in the line of sight, ... ought to be shot. . . .etc.
> Or in a billiard room, your opponent has made a break of eight, and looks as if he may be going to make eight more. If two or more people are present they are likely not to be especially interested in the game, and quietly talking perhaps. Or moving teacups or glasses. Simulate annoyance, *on your opponent's behalf,* with the onlookers.
>
> From *Gamesmanship* by Stephen Potter, Hart-Davis 1947
> Reprinted by permission of A D Peters and Co Ltd

For discussion

1 Potter's rules of gamesmanship are part-joke, part-serious. Can you think of any occasions when you yourself have employed similar devices to win over your opponent? (The setting might not necessarily be a sporting event.) What happened?
2 Sometimes we demoralise our opponents without meaning to do so. Can you think of an example from your own experience?
3 A good salesman is often also a good 'gamesman', employing all sorts of tricks and techniques (without actually cheating) in order to achieve a sale. Think of a situation in which (a) the salesman is the skilful

'gamesman'. Then think of (b) the situation in which the would-be buyer is the gamesman. Then think of (c) the situation in which *both* are masters of gamesmanship.

4 Devise other rules of gamesmanship in addition to the two quoted in the extract above, and improvise scenes to illustrate them in operation.

* * *

Structured improvisation

This is for three characters, Walker, Smith and Shuter. They are candidates for a history scholarship to an Oxford college, and all three are at present in the sixth form of various secondary schools. They have not met before. The setting is a waiting-room at the college (say, Christchurch). They are the same age, and they have all been highly recommended by their schools, and have taken a written examination at the College.

All three can suppose that they have done well in the written exam, and that is why they have been invited to the interview. At the interview they will be facing half a dozen tutors of the College, and they will be asked various things about their school careers, and about their knowledge of history, and about the essays they have written for the examination. Presumably, other candidates have also been invited to the interview, but the three of you, at this moment, can only see each other: there are no other students in the waiting room. In fact, as the scene begins, Walker has been waiting for ten minutes, and Smith walks in as the next person on the interviews' list. Shuter is inside the interview room, and he comes out from the interview a few minutes *after* the scene begins. You can assume that all of you are keen to win the scholarship, and all of you are very nervous. You can also safely assume that you will not wish to show your nervousness or your keenness to each other.

Instructions for WALKER *(alone):* you have a very competitive nature, and are determined to win this scholarship and to demoralise any possible rival. You saw Shuter just before he went in for the interview, and are outraged that he is so long inside the room. When he does eventually come out, you will find some way of demoralising him — perhaps by saying that you'd heard they keep the good candidates much longer, or even, that you'd heard they keep the good candidates no time at all. But you have an armoury of tactics for demoralising others. They include: what school do you go to? (you go to a second rate public school, but will represent this as better than Eton or Harrow.) Did your parents go to this college? (your father did). Do you play rugby? are you very good at it? (you will imply that poor rugby players never get into this college) Do you have to spend much time reading books before you understand them? (you will imply you understand everything at once) — and will add to the list of techniques as you go on. The rivals you meet in the waiting-room present you with a marvellous opportunity for demoralising them, and you will seize this readily.

Instructions for SMITH *(alone):* you are especially nervous, because you have never been before to an Oxford college, nor do you know anybody else who has done so. You attend a local comprehensive high school, and are a leading pupil there, but you feel out of your depth here, though you would never dream of showing it. You are very unsure about the kind of questions you are likely to be asked, and you would appreciate some guidance on this matter.

Instructions for SHUTER *(alone):* you have had a gruelling interview, and they have asked you some of the toughest questions (on your essays) that you have ever had to face. They were quite charming, but cool. You yourself started out with very little confidence, because the chap who was interviewed *before* you (and who will now have gone home) told you, in a hushed voice, that they had already decided to give the scholarship to a particularly brilliant candidate from Harrow. He'd heard this from a friend who's already a student at the College, and who had heard this from his own tutor. But they did give you a long interview, and so that's encouraging, perhaps. You are at Eton, and are considered a good scholar, and you would quite like the scholarship to Christchurch, but you are not absolutely sure of this. There is a part of you that would rather give up study altogether, and travel.

As you leave the interview, the Principal of the College asks you (a) to wait in the waiting room, since they may wish to call you back, and (b) to tell those who are waiting that there will be a break of ten minutes while the interviewing board have coffee.

19 Learning

When we come to school for the first time, we already know a great deal. But, occasionally, teachers are faced with pupils who appear to know absolutely nothing — cannot speak even. This was the case when the Frenchman *Jean Itard* undertook to educate a boy named Victor who had been captured wild in a forest, and who appeared never to have had any contact with human beings in his entire life. He seemed to be in his early adolescence. Victor was taken to Paris and put on show, but was soon pronounced an incurable idiot because he did not at once learn to talk and to do 'civilised' things. He would have been committed to an asylum but for Itard's offer to take the boy and help him. Itard kept a detailed diary of the boy's progress, and Victor did eventually learn a great deal. Itard educated him entirely on his own. The only other person allowed on the scene was the housekeeper.

Itard attempted to teach Victor everything (with varied success) — including a sense of right and wrong. One of his difficulties, since the boy's language developed slowly and unsurely, was in knowing when he had succeeded. In this extract he attempts to punish the boy for something he has *not* done, and thereby to teach him that people can be unfair and unjust:

> For this truly painful experience, I chose a day when Victor and I had been working together for more than a couple of hours and when his intelligence and obedience were such that I had only praises and rewards to offer him. To judge from the contented expression on his face he was clearly expecting them. Imagine his astonishment when, instead, I put on a severe and threatening expression, rubbed out what I had just praised and scattered all his books and cards around the room. Finally I seized him by the arm and dragged him roughly towards a little dark room which had sometimes served him as a prison when he first came to Paris. He put up no resistance until we got as far as the threshold, then suddenly coming out of his usual submissive state, he put hands and feet against the door posts and set up the most vigorous resistance. This pleased me immeasurably because it was something totally new for him; for when faced by a just punishment,

he had always endured it without the slightest air of rebellion. I carried on with my plan, however, as I wished to see how far he would persist in his resistance. Beside himself with indignation and scarlet with rage, he struggled in my arms, until finally he threw himself on my hand and bit it long and hard. At that moment I would have given anything to be able to make my pupil understand my act, for the bite was a legitimate act of vengeance. It was an incontestable proof that the idea of justice and injustice, was no longer foreign to my pupil's mind. By giving this feeling to him, or rather by stimulating its development, I had raised savage man to the full stature of moral man....

From *The Wild Boy of Aveyron* by Jean Itard, translated by Lucien Malson, NLB

For discussion

1 Itard saw this as a way of teaching the boy a sense of justice. Do you think he succeeded as he thought he did?
2 What other ways might a teacher employ for the same purpose?
3 How do you think you yourself have learned a sense of justice? — And can you think of a particular incident which more than almost anything else has given you a strong sense of right and wrong? What happened?
4 Itard set up an artificial situation, and, in effect, play-acted in front of and to his student, without letting the student know (until later, presumably). Compare Itard's technique with the teacher in the following extract from an American magazine:

Elementary Schoolteacher Donna Kenzie is developing a new form of moral instruction with her second grade children, this year. She says it is highly productive of good results, and hopes other teachers will be encouraged to use it.
Donna's method is to set up situations where children are unjustly treated, and then to help them to understand what has happened and why.
'Last week I was very unfriendly to one little girl for no reason at all. This went on all afternoon, and some of the other children started being unfriendly to her as well. Then I told them I had only been play-acting, and I hadn't any reason for what I'd done. This made them all see that they hadn't any reason either, and they all felt bad for being so bad to her. This way, I can set up situations where the children can see right and wrong from things that are actually going on, there and then, in the classroom!'

What do you think of Donna Kenzie's technique?

What are any of the possible dangers in this technique?
Devise a situation in which a teacher tries the same basic method with older pupils. Improvise it.
Devise and improvise a situation in which pupils try the same method with the teacher.

* * *

Lucy wants an apple

Sometimes, those who are learning, and those who are teaching them, give up all hope of success. The following extract should, therefore, give hope to all of us:

> A few years ago, in the small town of Norman, Oklahoma, a reporter from 'The New York Times' had a brief conversation with a little girl called Lucy.
> He held up a key and asked, 'What is this?'
> 'Key,' Lucy replied.
> Then he picked up a comb: 'What's this?'
> 'Comb,' answered Lucy, as she took it from his hands and proceeded to comb his hair. She stopped.
> 'Comb me,' she pleaded.
> 'OK,' he said, and combed her.
> 'Lucy, you want to go outside?' he suggested.
> She thought for a while and then replied: 'Outside, no. Want food — apple.'
> 'I have no food,' he apologised. 'sorry.'
>
> A singularly unremarkable dialogue, one might think; indeed the girl seemed rather backward in her grammar. But the conversation was not *spoken*; it was conducted with a series of hand movements, in American sign language for the deaf. Lucy is not deaf, however; she is a chimpanzee with human fosterparents. . .
>
> Two American psychologists, Allen and Beatrice Gardner, started the project in Nevada in 1966. The first scholar in their academy for apes was a one-year-old chimpanzee called Washoe, whom they kept in a luxurious caravan, surrounded by obsequious attendants who constantly talked to her and to each other in hand language. By the age of five, Washoe had learned the gestural signs for nearly 200 words, including adjectives and verbs as well as nouns. (Also, both Washoe and Lucy) have spontaneously invented a few signs of their own. Washoe for example, signalled for her bib by drawing its outline on her chest. And Lucy used her own invented word for the halter that she has

to wear during walks: she mimes the act of putting on the leash, and often precedes it by the gesture for 'dirty', just to indicate her disgust at having to wear it.

Even more interesting is the way in which Washoe and Lucy couple their limited stocks of words together, to manufacture new ones. According to Lucy, a water-melon is a 'drink-fruit' or a 'candy-drink', and a strong radish is 'cry-hurt-food'. And even though she has been taught a single gesture for refrigerator, Washoe prefers to call it an 'open-food-drink'. Is this true linguistic resourcefulness, approaching the human use of language...?

From *A Burning Fire* the BBC Reith Lectures 1976 by Colin Blakemore
Cambridge University Press 1977

For discussion
1 Man's capacity to learn and to use language, is usually considered his distinguishing feature. No other species can do this. How far does the work with the chimpanzees demolish this idea?
2 What limitations do you think there are to their possible progress?
3 Few people would have expected the chimpanzees to do so well. Can you think of any instance from your own experience where someone has made totally unexpected progress in learning something? What happened?
4 The two psychologists showed great resourcefulness in finding ways of teaching their pupils. Find a similar instance of resourcefulness among teachers (real or imaginary) and improvise it.
5 The extract could just possibly be the beginning of a highly dramatic story, perhaps even of a piece of 'science fiction'. Devise such a story, and choose some incidents to improvise.

20 Whodunit?

Structured improvisation

Instructions for ALL THE CHARACTERS: earlier this evening, the Cranshaws gave a small dinner party. Eric Cranshaw has recently started work as a junior executive with Goddards Ltd, an advertising agency, and the dinner was intended to introduce himself and his wife to other members of the firm. During the dinner, conversation ranged over many topics, including a red diamond ring which Mrs Cranshaw was wearing. After dinner, the men smoked and drank in the dining room while the ladies did the washing-up in the kitchen. During the washing-up the ladies cleared everything off the dining-room table except for a vase of flowers which was left in the centre. The ladies also brought some of the crockery back into the dining room and placed it inside the china-cabinet. Then Mrs Cranshaw screamed out that her ring was missing. The kitchen and dining-room were thoroughly searched, and then, since Mrs Cranshaw was now hysterical, Mr Cranshaw called the police. A Detective-Inspector arrived, and after ascertaining roughly what had happened he decided to interview all the members of the dinner party privately. One of the guests, Mr Cross, suggested that it would be much easier simply to have everyone searched, but the Inspector rejected this suggestion.

The layout of the ground floor is as follows: the entrance-hall leads into the dining-room and into a lounge and into a toilet; the dining-room leads into the kitchen.

Improvise the Interviews and the Inspector's Report. The members of the dinner party are: *Eric Cranshaw,* host, aged 30. *Ellen Cranshaw,* his wife, aged 27. *John Baldock,* 55, Managing Director of Goddards Ltd. *Kay Baldock,* 50, his wife. *Stanley Cross,* 31, a Junior Executive of Goddards Ltd. A bachelor. *Stella Larkwood,* 35, spinster, assistant chief accountant at Goddards Ltd. *Detective-Inspector.* (He could be the whole class, acting as a team of inquiry)

Instructions for THE INSPECTOR: make notes on any details that you think important. Be very polite to all the people you interview, and do not at any moment betray any suspicions that you may form. You can, if you choose, after interviewing everyone, ask to re-interview particular people. Your questions should be designed to ascertain roughly what each person was doing at about the time the ring was stolen, and whether anything that is said conflicts significantly with other people's accounts. At the end of the interviews you should present your report, verbally, to your superiors (the rest of the group) and indicate clearly who, if at all, you consider the guilty party, and why.

You could always, of course, ask everyone to agree to being searched, but you are fully aware that by this time if anyone has stolen the ring then they would have disposed of it before you arrived. Also, all the guests have expressed a perfect willingness to co-operate with you, and this again suggests that the ring has already been disposed of. You have, however, given orders to two of your men to search the house for any signs of the ring. They conduct a very thorough search, but no ring is discovered.

Instructions for ERIC CRANSHAW: aged 30. Married three years. Appointed Junior Executive at Goddards three weeks ago. Your wife Ellen was very delighted with your appointment and suggested the dinner party as a way of getting to know the people you work with, and as a way of helping you to achieve promotion later on. Your wife is somewhat scatter-brained, and has already lost two rings which you bought her, though neither of those was worth very much. The insurance companies have refused to re-insure your wife's rings, and so you stand no chance of getting back the value of the missing ring, which is worth £500 and is an old family ring handed on to your wife by your own grandmother. You were enjoying the dinner party, which seemed a great success, and your first reaction when the ring was reported missing was to think that your wife had simply put it down and forgotten where. but she insists that she left it on the dining-room table before she started to do the washing-up. To do this, she must either have taken off the ring before going from the dining-room into the kitchen, or else have returned from the kitchen into the dining-room after she had cleared the dinner things away. She claims that she did it after she had actually started to wash up, and that she was advised to take the ring off by Mrs Baldock, the wife of your managing director, who like Stella Larkwood, the accountant, helped Ellen with the washing-up, while Mr Baldock, Stanley Cross (your fellow Junior Executive) and yourself sat smoking and drinking at the dining-room table. You cannot remember seeing the ring anywhere except on your wife's finger. It is not a ring that she often wears. You can remember that there was some conversation about the ring earlier in the evening. Mrs Baldock commented on it during the dinner, and everyone admired it, and Stanley Cross commented that it must be 'worth a fortune'.

You have found all your guests extremely good humoured about this whole unfortunate business — they have been most understanding about your wife's hysterical outburst when she discovered the loss of the ring, and the Baldocks have been exceptionally kind — and so this has confirmed your belief that your wife is herself to blame, and that she has lost it, quite probably down the sink, while washing-up.

Instructions for ELLEN CRANSHAW: aged 27, married three years. Husband recently appointed Junior Executive at an advertising firm, Goddards Ltd. You were delighted at this appointment, and you suggested the dinner party to him as a way of enhancing his social standing in the firm. Everyone tells you that you are rather scatter-brained, though you never quite see why. You are occasionally careless, and have in fact lost two other rings which your husband gave you, but they were not very valuable ones and you have more or less forgotten about them. Because of the loss of those two rings, both of which were insured, the insurance companies have refused to re-insure the last remaining ring, which is worth £500 and was given to you (as a family heirloom) by your husband's grandmother. You are desperate at the loss of this ring. And you remember very clearly what happened to the ring in the course of the evening. You wore the ring for the first time in over a year, and both Mrs Baldock and Stella Larkwood (the accountant) commented on it, and admired it. Someone, one of the men probably, ventured to say that it must be worth a great deal of money. After dinner, Mrs Baldock said that she would help you with the washing-up, though you had intended to leave it until the guests had left. But Mrs Baldock insisted, and so rather than offend her — she is after all, the wife of your husband's employer — you agreed to let her help you. Stella Larkwood also said that she would help you, and the three of you cleared the things into the kitchen while the men started to smoke around the table. You were already washing-up when one of the women, probably Stella Larkwood, advised you not to wear the ring while you were at the sink. So as to be completely sure that the ring didn't get mixed up with the washing-up things, you went back into the dining-room and left the ring in a prominent position on the table. At that particular moment, as you remember it, the men were around the cocktail cabinet pouring out drinks and hardly noticed you. While you were washing-up, both Stella Larkwood and Mrs Baldock went into the dining-room a couple of times to put various pieces of crockery into the china-cabinet.

When you went back into the dining-room and discovered that the ring was missing, you nearly fainted. Then you became hysterical, for you were well aware that someone had taken it. You are deeply sorry that the dinner party should have ended so badly, but are desperate to have the ring back.

You do not suspect anyone. You have found both the ladies charming, especially Mrs Baldock, and the men have been equally courteous and good natured.

Instructions for JOHN BALDOCK: aged 55, managing director of Goddards Ltd. Married thirty years to Kay Baldock. Two children, one at school, one in the Navy. You have known for many years now that your wife is a kleptomaniac, but you love her dearly and have protected her and covered up for her with amazing skill and success. Nobody else knows. She only ever steals small things, though they are also often very valuable. Always steals things of no practical use to herself, and always loses interest in the things quite soon after stealing them. In the present instance, you and nobody else saw Mrs Cranshaw place the ring on the dining-room table just before she started to do the washing-up, and then you saw your wife a little later come in to put some crockery away in a cabinet, pick up the ring from the table and put it away in her handbag. At the first opportunity you went over to your wife's handbag, on a pretext of looking for a cigarette, and removed the ring. You very carefully put it back on the table.

To your astonishment, five minutes later, Mrs Cranshaw screamed out that the ring was missing.

You have no idea what could have happened. But you suspect your wife, and hope very much that she will not be found out.

You are a well-liked employer, and have the respect and goodwill of your employees. You are quite impressed with young Cranshaw, and think he will do well. You have recently helped out Stella Larkwood, the assistant accountant, with a large loan, interest free, to help out her younger brother who has got into serious financial scrapes.

Instructions for KAY BALDOCK: aged 50, wife of John Baldock. Married thirty years, two children, one at school, one in the Navy. Devoted to your husband, who is a brilliantly successful business man. You have for some years now suffered from an unaccountable urge to steal. Have often stolen small but valuable things for which you personally have had no use, but have never yet been found out. On the occasion in question you noticed Ellen Cranshaw's ring when you were at dinner, and commented on it, and you gathered that it was worth a great deal of money. After dinner you offered to help with the washing-up, and this gave you a golden opportunity: you advised Ellen to take the ring off while she was at the sink, saw her take it off and place it on the dining-room table, and so at the earliest opportunity you went into the dining-room to put some crockery away into the china-cabinet, saw the men pre-occupied at the drinks cabinet, and took the ring and placed it in your handbag. At least you think you did, for incredibly enough a few minutes later you saw it back again on the table, lying alongside a bowl of flowers. So you scooped up the bowl of flowers and the ring with it and placed the flowers on the china-cabinet and held the ring for the moment in the palm of your hand. You are extremely skilful at this sort of thing, and enjoy the advantage that nobody ever guesses for one instant that you could ever so much as dream of committing a crime of any kind. You got back into the kitchen just as Ellen cried out that her ring had disappeared. Realising that the situation had become dangerous you went straight into the toilet that adjoins the hall and dropped the ring down the cistern and pulled the chain. A few moments later you rejoined the party, and expressed great sympathy for Ellen's predicament and suggested that she had probably left it in the kitchen.

You are a skilled liar, and have no intention that anyone should know of what you have done!

Instructions for STANLEY CROSS: aged 31. Junior Executive of Goddards Ltd for the past seven years. Bachelor. You enjoyed the dinner party and can remember the ladies chatting about the ring Mrs Cranshaw was wearing. Such things don't interest you. You remember that the ladies insisted on helping Mrs Cranshaw with the washing-up while Mr Baldock, Cranshaw and yourself poured out drinks from the cocktail cabinet in the dining-room and discussed all sorts of general topics – the world situation, golf, taxation and so on. You can remember that the women kept on popping back into the dining-room from the kitchen to put things away in the china-cabinet. You can remember only one slightly odd thing about the proceedings: at one moment Mrs Baldock, your employer's wife, a most charming lady, removed a vase of flowers from the dining-room table on to the china-cabinet, and seconds later Stella Larkwood, the highly efficient assistant accountant at your office, moved the flowers back on to the table. At about that time you heard Mrs Cranshaw screaming out that the ring was missing.

Instructions for STELLA LARKWOOD: spinster, aged 35. Assistant to the Chief Accountant at Goddards Ltd. Hard worker; well qualified. You live with your widowed mother. Have always helped your family, and recently, when your younger brother incurred a very large gambling debt, you asked your boss, Mr Baldock, if he would lend you the necessary money. He did so, and this was typical of him, for he is a most generous man, and is always willing to help people who are in difficulties. You feel a great loyalty towards him, and for this reason you never told a single person when you discovered that his wife, Mrs Baldock, is a kleptomaniac. You first made this discovery when she stole a rather attractive powder-compact from your handbag some years ago at the office. Since then you have several times seen her steal things, and on one embarrassing occasion she took you shopping with her, and proceeded to steal several quite useless items from various shop counters. On this occasion, you remember chatting about the ring over dinner, and remember Mrs Baldock advising Mrs Cranshaw to take the ring off before doing the washing-up. When you had finished helping the two ladies with the washing-up you helped to put some of the things back into the china-cabinet, and at that moment you saw Mrs Baldock quietly scoop up the vase of flowers on the dining-room table, and you think you saw her pick up the ring which was lying alongside it. She placed the vase on the china-cabinet, and almost at that moment Mrs Cranshaw screamed out that the ring was missing. Mrs Baldock went back into the kitchen, and you guessed that she might have dropped the ring into the vase in order to rid herself of it. So you picked up the vase, almost without thinking about it, intending to look inside it, but you realised that you couldn't immediately look in the vase without attracting suspicion. So you casually put the vase down again where Mrs Cranshaw had first placed it, on the dining-room table.

You have no intention of betraying Mrs Baldock, and you realise that you are the only one who knows what has actually happened. To the best of your knowledge Mr Baldock is not aware of his wife's various thefts.

Adapted from author's earlier book, *Improvised Drama*, Batsford 1967

21 Friendship

(See also section 2 for the 'younger' group)

Preliminary Pages for a Work of Revenge

    The characters in this work are meant to be real. Reference to persons living and dead are intended.

    Are there fifteen people in the world who will be afraid when they read this paragraph? No. That in itself is a comment on my insignificance. Are there fifteen people who will become uneasy on reading it? I think so.... I know some things about some of them which they would not like to see written down...

    The author does not wish to express his gratitude to anyone. He has no reason to be grateful. He does, however, wish to acknowledge that parts of this work have been provided him unwittingly by relatives and friends, enemies and acquaintances. The uses he intends to make of the facts, lies, rumours, scandals and secrets so provided shall be his own....

    So — about the author:
I am that person you insulted. I am that person you forgot. I am the one you do not speak of, the person you hope never to meet again. I am the one you said something mean and spiteful about and I have heard what you said. I am that friend who fell out of fashion, whose reminiscences about old times you found boring, whose dinner invitation you did not return, whose address you did not keep. I am that person you never phoned back. I am that person you flattered then ignored, the one who rang your doorbell many times while you sat like a statue inside, hoping I would go away. I am the one whose footsteps you heard going down the stairs, who never knew you were there and hated you for it....

    I am that person you betrayed....

From *'Preliminary Pages for a Work of Revenge'* by Brian Moore from *Canadian Writing Today*, Penguin 1970

For discussion

1 Most of us at some time seek revenge, or dream secretly of seeking it. What kinds of things lead us to be 'vengeful'?

2 Do we feel guilty about our desire for revenge? Should we?
3 It is often difficult to keep an even balance between the injury itself, and the thing we do by way of having our revenge. Can you think of an example of this, perhaps from your own experience?
4 Take the last line from the extract, and devise the story that follows it. Write it. Improvise an incident from it.
5 (Following on from 4) imagine that the written story falls into the hands of someone who knows the participants or is in the story. Devise a sequel showing what happens next.
6 In the extract, friends are identified as objects for revenge. Is this credible? Do we change from friends into enemies? How does this happen? Can you given an example, from fact or fiction?

* * *

Master and disciple

In the late nineteenth century, *Sigmund Freud* laid the foundations of psycho-analysis — a technique in which specially trained doctors listen to the reminiscences and life-stories of people who have reached some kind of mental/nervous breakdown, and then analyse these stories to help the patient see and understand what has happened. Freud worked in Vienna, and attracted a large number of students, followers and disciples. Among them was a former lawyer named *Victor Tausk*, who worked for and with Freud and then, finally, committed suicide. The reason for his self-destruction seems partly to have been a feeling of failure and rejection when Freud repeatedly kept him out of the charmed circle of his closest friends.

One possible reason why Freud excluded Tausk was that he feared Tausk as a rival; especially, he may have feared that Tausk would claim responsibilities for some of Freud's own discoveries. Tausk, was in a sense, a possible plagiarist — someone who takes another's invention/creation and represents it as his own:

> Freud felt uncomfortable with someone like Tausk around, a man bright enough even to anticipate some of his own concepts. Freud did not like the uncertainty lest Tausk have an idea before he did. And it bothered Freud to have to acknowledge Tausk's contributions. . . .
> The whole issue of plagiarism bothers all who write. Can anyone ever feel he has fully acknowledged all his intellectual debts? Do not students sometimes fail to acknowledge the leads of their teachers? People might quote Freud, but not in the right places. Freud still had discoveries to make, but he might make them so convincingly that Tausk

could believe he had thought of them first. Tausk could then elaborate Freud's concepts with his own clinical material, without making the distinction between what was his and what was Freud's.
Even creative writers have been beset by this anxiety. Hemingway, for example, said that he 'always had that problem — other writers pinching my stuff.' In science, it becomes a matter of the greatest importance who first makes a discovery. Was it Darwin or Wallace who discovered evolution through natural selection?
What is worse the most likely channels of plagiarism are not conscious. .

Shortly before killing himself, Tausk wrote to Freud:

Dear Professor,
Please excuse my absence from today's meeting. I am occupied in solving the decisive affairs of my life and I do not want by contact with you to be tempted to resort to your help. I shall probably soon be free again to approach you. In the meantime I remain with cordial, respectful regards, gratefully yours,
Tausk.

From *Brother Animal: the story of Freud and Tausk* by Paul Roazen, Penguin 1970

For discussion
1 In a case like this, to what extent is one friend responsible for the other friend's predicament?
2 You could say of a case like this, that rivalry destroyed friendship. Can you think of any other instance where this happened — whether real or imaginary, fact or fiction?
3 Freud was afraid of plagiarism. Devise a situation in which you might yourself experience the same fear. Improvise it.
4 Tausk's letter to Freud gives no indication of his state of mind and his probable intention. Think of a situation in which two people write a short series of letters to each other, in which the intentions of one or both of them are hinted at but do not really come to the surface. Write it, as a story. Take an incident from it, and improvise it.

* * *

Structured improvisation

For two characters, Hammond and Lowe: these are both aeronautical engineers. Hammond is a leading research engineer, working for a major aircraft company. Lowe is rather younger, and came to Hammond as an assistant two years ago. You have been working together on an ambitious research programme designed to measure and predict the durability of aircraft such as Concorde and Boeings 707 and 747. Of course, a great deal of knowledge on this subject already exists, but your own research project, instigated by Hammond, is expected to produce some dramatically new discoveries in this field. In effect, the research is concerned with the general field of fatigue and stress on the bodies of aircraft when in flight, and so with the general question of how long they can safely be expected to fly. *In this scene*, Lowe has asked to see Hammond to discuss some recent development in his work. They meet in Hammond's office.

Instructions for LOWE: you are a brilliant aeronautical engineer, and know that you could obtain work, highly paid, anywhere in the world. Offers constantly come to you from the U.S.A., but you have refused, so far, to join the brain drain. You started on the research project with a great admiration for Hammond, who is quite well known and distinguished, but you have been repeatedly and increasingly disappointed with his work, and with working under him. He seems to you completely self-centred, and so caught up in his own ambition to produce interesting and important research that you are given no credit for your own ideas and are given no chance ever to take the limelight. You wanted to work on a project where your own thinking and your own ideas would have equal weight with everybody else's, but this is not the case with Hammond. So you have decided to make a break, and take your services elsewhere. You recently met a brilliant American Professor called Flenheim, who was touring this country. He runs an enormous department of aeronautical engineering in Michigan. He invited you, in a very informal way, to go out and visit him any time. You have decided to do so. You are convinced that this means he will give you a job once you are out there. But you do not wish to lose your present job until you have definitely another to go to, so you will not give in your notice here. You will simply ask for immediate leave of absence for say, four weeks.

Instructions for HAMMOND: you have been pleased with Lowe. He works well, and has helped you considerably. In your research, you have just made a breakthrough. If you work hard and without interruption for the next four weeks, you will achieve the results you have been working for. But you are deeply afraid that the praise and acknowledgment for all your years of hard work will, at this final moment, be taken away from you. This could happen *either* through the 'defection' of one of your assistants (such as Lowe) who runs off and claims the credit for what you have done, *or* through the espionage of a rival who finds out your discovery and claims it as his own before you have published it. You are especially afraid that the American, Flenheim, a professor from Michigan, who came snooping round your project quite recently, has got spies somewhere on the scene, and so you will take special care that no friends of Flenheim get anywhere near your work for the next week or two. As regards Lowe, you decide that the right thing to do is to tell him nothing of your discoveries, and to mislead him into thinking that you are getting nowhere. You will sound him out to see if he knows anything about what you have been doing, and provided he knows as little as you think he knows, you will invent a new project to involve him until you are ready to unveil your own achievement.

22 Whose Responsibility?

Many children battered but neighbours stay silent
The reluctance of neighbours, friends and relatives to tell the authorities is leaving hundreds of children to be battered at home by their parents, the National Society for the Prevention of Cruelty to Children suggests in its annual report published today.

Some children 'were terribly disfigured by assaults of incredible ferocity,' the report said. Some were 'starved and neglected to a degree that is unthinkable in a civilised community.'
'We are convinced that many more children are suffering needlessly, yet those who know of their circumstances choose to remain silent.'

For discussion
1. Why do you think neighbours and friends are so reluctant to reveal such happenings? Why do they 'choose to remain silent'?
2. In a similar situation, would you yourself speak up? Would you report such a thing?
3. Imagine a situation in which a social worker discovers a case of extreme neglect or cruelty to a child. How might (a) the parents and (b) other people such as relatives, etc., explain their actions (or their lack of action)?
4. Have you yourself ever 'stayed silent' when someone else is mistreated? Have others stayed silent when you were mistreated? What happened?
5. It is often difficult to know whether or not we should interfere to help others, or whether we have any sort of right to do so. Can you think of any occasion when such a problem might arise in everyday life? or when it has arisen in your own experience?

* * *

Sometimes we tell ourselves that we are not to blame for what happens as a result of our actions, because other people in the same situation are generally held not to blame. As an example:

In 1947, fifteen German doctors, distinguished medical men at the very top of their profession, were convicted by the Nuremberg war crimes tribunal of criminal responsibility for cruel and murderous medical experiments performed on concentration camp inmates. Seven of these doctors were sentenced to death by hanging, others to long terms of imprisonment. In their defence the doctors quoted the many experiments carried out by American doctors on ordinary prisoners in American jails. In general, these experiments have been designed to test new drugs on 'live' prisoners, before releasing them for normal use among the population. Such experiments still go on in the USA, and perhaps elsewhere. In one recent case, a prisoner who refused to take part in such an experiment was held down by force, injected with a drug, and later developed a near-fatal disease. It is perfectly possible that many such prisoners have died as a result of such experiments, though no official statement has ever confirmed this.

Prisoners are usually offered a reward of some kind if they will volunteer for these experiments. The reward may be a few dollars in cash, or a reduction in their prison sentence. The drug companies and the doctors receive massive financial rewards when the experiment proves successful and the new drug can be profitably put on the market.

Material in this article taken from *The American Prison Business* by Jessica Mitford, Allen and Unwin 1974

For discussion
1. What is there to be said in favour of such experiments?
2. What is there to be said against them?
3. Is there any parallel between this problem and the use of live animals for similar experiments?
4. Why is it possible to perform such experiments on prisoners? — why not on other sectors of the population?
5. Think of any situation in which you have managed to square something with your conscience, even though you have felt strongly that you were in the wrong. What happened? Improvise part of the incident.

* * *

Sometimes we become responsible for other people, simply by being generous and good-hearted. A charity can easily become a duty. Here is an example:

People frequently avoid giving assistance to the poor, for fear that once they have taken care of them they will always have them on their hands. It is a very common experience that the beggars to whom alms are given with regularity, consider these very rapidly as their right and as the duty of the giver, and if the latter fails in this supposed obligation they interpret it as a denial of their due contribution and feel a bitterness which they would not feel against someone who always denied them alms. There is also the person in better circumstance who has supported for some time a needy person, fixing in advance the period for which he will do so, and who, when he stops the gifts, is left with a painful feeling of guilt. This simple fact is recognised by an Indian law according to which he who has three times assisted a poor person with the same amount, thereby acquires the obligation of continuing with it. His act assumes the character of a vow, from which only weighty reasons can dispense him, such as, for example, his own impoverishment.

From 'The Poor' by George Simmel from *Individuality and Social Forms*, University of Chicago Press 1971

For discussion

1 Can you see how the Indian law in question might have grown up? Do you agree with it?
2 Can you think of an instance in which you have yourself come to accept someone's charity as a right to which you are fully entitled? What happened?
3 Note that the Indian law referred to, requires *three* successive gifts. Devise a story showing the operation of such a law. Give it a local everyday setting, and improvise it.

* * *

Are we responsible for our own actions?

In general, we think of it as common sense to accept responsibility for our own actions, and others, likewise, are responsible for what they do. But there are exceptions. People who are insane, people who are very drunk, people acting under the influence of drugs, for example, are usually considered by the law as not entirely responsible for what they do.

Sometimes it is difficult to draw the line between those situations where we should be, and those where we should not be, held responsible. Consider these problems:

1 A group of boys/girls at school in the playground. They get involved in a punch-up, with one pushing another, and a fight breaking out. One boy gets seriously hurt. Would you hold all of them responsible?

Whose Responsibility?

Have you ever been involved in such a situation? What happened? Who was to blame?

2 An older brother/sister and a younger brother/sister get involved in some kind of shop-lifting/theft. The parents blame the older, and say that he/she 'led' or 'misled' the younger one. Would you agree?
Have you ever been caught up in such an incident? What happened? Who was to blame?

3 An older child is regularly told to look after a younger one. The older one forgets his responsibilities for a moment, and during that time the younger one has an accident. Is the older one to blame?

4 A child is bullied and terrorised by a gang. They force the child to steal an old lady's handbag as she is walking out of the Post Office after collecting her old age pension. The child's parents say he/she is in no way to blame. Do you agree?

5 In 1976 a wealthy American girl, Patty Hearst, aged 21, was charged with armed bank robbery. She was found guilty. Her defence was that she had been kidnapped by a group of terrorists and forced to take part in the gang's criminal acts. The court accepted that Hearst had been violently treated by the gang, but nevertheless held that she was responsible for her own actions and, therefore, for her involvement in the robbery, which had been organised by the gang. Would you agree that in such cases, an accused person is responsible?

Take any one of the above situations, and use it as a basis for improvisation.

23 Starting Work

The following are comments from various young people who have recently left school and started work:

> I couldn't wait to leave. I learnt nothing at school. Just 'do as you're told'.

> School was bad enough, but work's worse. I tell you — it's over-rated.

> Work — ? There's nothing to it. Just as boring as school, but they *pay* you. Not much. But it's something. And you're someone!

> It's funny to say so, but I miss school. Already I miss it. I'm in an office and there's only five other people besides myself. And they're all right. But there was so much more to do at school.

> I don't know anything. I really don't. And I've only just realised it. I'm SO IGNORANT. I don't know whose fault it is. Mine? My teachers? My mates?

> I was scared stiff the day I started work. Just as bad as the day I started school when I was five. Only this time I didn't have my mum walking up to the gates with me, holding my hand. I was so scared I'd make a fool of myself. And I did.

> They don't really get you ready for work, not when you're at school. I don't mean teaching you the right subjects, I mean teaching you how to behave, what to do and what to say. I felt so awkward when I started work. It was agony. I still feel it, really.

> I suppose the work's boring, in a way. I suppose in another ten years if I'm still doing it, I'll be fed up. But I still like it better than school. They treat you better. You're an equal, in a way.

> I liked school. I like work. But it's routine what I do. Doesn't need any initiative. Perhaps if I'd worked harder at school I'd have got a better job. Perhaps I could have studied and gone to college. My brother did. But he got fed up at college. He dropped out. My parents were mad with him. Maybe that's why they didn't really bother so much about me.

For discussion

1 Do any of these comments 'ring true'?

2 What are your own fears, if any, about starting work?
3 Several of the comments refer to the stresses and strains of the first few days at work, and especially to the general feeling of embarrassment at not quite knowing what to do. Have you heard any stories from other people who have actually experienced this? What happened?
4 Take an incident from such a story and improvise it.

* * *

Jobs wanted

Sometimes people advertise their services, so that prospective employers can write in. Here are two examples:

1 Intelligent, gifted, wasted young woman, having lavished the best years of her life on the typewriter and Mr Pitman's shorthand, seeks exciting outlet for fresh start. Anything legal considered. Wages not prime consideration, but must be adequate. Write Box....
2 Dangerous young man seeks dangerous employment. Anything considered. Write Box....

And sometimes, of course, employers advertise in similar terms:

1 Company director requires intelligent secretary, able to cope with busy schedule and hectic routine. Salary — nothing but the best for the one for whom nothing is too much. Write Box....
2 An opportunity occurs for one or more intelligent young men to learn the wine trade and further their education in South West France. Qualifications: reasonable GCE standard or higher, pleasant personality, and ability to play good club rugby.

1 Take any one of these adverts and devise a situation in which the advertisement is answered and the two parties, employee and employer, come to meet each other.
2 Take any one of these adverts and use it as the start of an adventure story. What happens next?
3 *Watch this outer space for job*

In 1980 the European Space Agency Spacelab will blast off from Cape Kennedy, Florida, carrying two astronauts, an American and a European. The European *could be you*, providing you meet the following specifications and are judged to be the most ideal applicant:
    measuring between 153 and 190 cm

excellent physical health
not more than 47 years old
willing to partake of life science experiments
   during flight
possessing degree in engineering or science
having five years' experience in solar physics or
   allied subject

From all the applicants, a short list of six will be selected. They will be interviewed, and an even shorter list of two will then be selected for the final interview.

What kinds of question are likely to be asked at the interviews? Is it possible that a person possessing all the necessary qualifications might not want to go? Improvise such a situation. The interview could easily be the start of a space fiction adventure story. Devise such a story, and improvise part of it.

* * *

Decline and Fall

Paul Pennyfeather is an innocent, naive young man, who is expelled from his Oxford college for 'indecent behaviour'. His offence, though, is simply to be attacked by a group of fellow-students, and to be left without his trousers in the college quadrangle. Unsure how to earn a living, he applies for a job teaching in a private school:

'Can you hear me quite clearly?' asked Dr Fagan.
'Perfectly, thank you.'
'Good; then let us get to business.'
Paul eyed him shyly across the table. He was very tall and very old and very well dressed; he had sunken eyes and rather long white hair over jet black eyebrows. His head was very long, and swayed lightly as he spoke; his voice had a thousand modulations, as though at some remote time he had taken lessons in elocution; the backs of his hands were hairy, and his fingers were crooked like claws.
'I understand you have had no previous experience?'
'No, sir, I am afraid not.'
'Well, of course, that is in many ways an advantage. One too easily acquires the professional tone and loses vision. But of course we must be practical. I am offering a salary of one hundred and twenty pounds, but only to a man with experience. . . . I understand too, that you left your University rather suddenly. Now — why was that?'
That was the question that Paul had been dreading, and true to his training, he had resolved upon honesty.
'I was sent down, sir, for indecent behaviour.'
'Indeed, indeed? Well, I shall not ask for details. I have been in the

scholastic profession long enough to know that nobody enters it unless he has some very good reason which he is anxious to conceal But, again to be practical, Mr Pennyfeather, I can hardly pay one hundred and twenty pounds to anyone who has been sent down for indecent behaviour. Suppose that we fix your salary at ninety pounds a year to begin with?'

'I have to return to Llanabba tonight. There are six more weeks of term, you see, and I have lost a master rather suddenly. I shall expect you tomorrow evening. There is an excellent train from Euston, that leaves at about ten.

'I think you will like your work,' he continued dreamily; 'you will find that my school is built upon an ideal — an ideal of service and fellowship. Little Lord Tangent has come to us this term, the Earl of Circumference's son, you know. Such a nice little chap, erratic, of course, like all his family, but he has *tone*.'

Dr Fagan gave a long sigh. 'I wish I could say the same for my staff. Between ourselves, Pennyfeather, I think I shall have to get rid of Grimes fairly soon. He is *not* out of the top drawer and boys notice these things. Now, your predecessor was a thoroughly agreeable young man. I was sorry to lose him. But he used to wake up my daughters coming back on his motor cycle at all hours of the night. He used to borrow money from the boys, too, quite large sums, and the parents objected. I had to get rid of him. . . . Still, I was very sorry. *He* had tone.'

Dr Fagan rose, put on his hat at a jaunty angle, and drew on a glove. 'Goodbye, my dear Pennyfeather. I think, in fact I know, that we are going to work well together. I can always tell these things.'

'Goodbye, sir,' said Paul.

From *Decline and Fall* by Evelyn Waugh, Penguin 1951

For discussion

1 What do you learn about Fagan from this interview?
2 What might happen next?
3 Several characters are briefly referred to in this scene: Little Lord Tangent; Grimes; 'your predecessor'. Devise incidents illustrating their behaviour at the school. Improvise the incidents.
4 Devise a parallel distuation, in which a young man/woman, applies for a job.
5 Divide the class into two groups. Group 1 devise a character who applies for a position as 'travelling companion' to a rich, elderly invalid. (The position is advertised in the personal column of *The Times*.) Group 2 devise the character who places the advertisement — not necessarily the same person as the elderly invalid.
Choose one person from each of the two groups, and improvise the interview.

24 Violence

What makes a young thug?

A recent study of the lives and attitudes of young deliquents in London, has produced some varied findings:

> delinquents who are caught and get convicted (whether put on probation or sent to prison) tend to commit more (and more serious) offences when they are released;
> delinquents who break the law and get away with it are more likely to behave better in the future;
> serious delinquents, thugs who will eventually cause great injury to someone or other, are in a minority, and they can be spotted at an early age;
> teachers should try to spot possible delinquents, and divert their activities into constructive leisure pursuits;
> young delinquents are most likely to reform when they leave home, and start to set up their own family; at such a time they are most receptive to outside help and advice;
> delinquents tend to break traffic rules more than non-delinquents, and to have more accidents;
> they tend to smoke, drink and gamble more than others;
> more prosecutions, and stiffer penalties do not necessarily solve the problem, or even alleviate it.

For discussion
1 Do any of these findings surprise you?
2 With reference to the first two items above, would you then recommend the police *not* to prosecute (or arrest)?
3 Why do you think we may commit more crimes, once we have been convicted of committing one?
4 Can you think of an instance where you did something wrong, and avoided the blame for it? What happened? What might have been the effect on you, if you had been found out?
5 Consider these questions:

Violence

Someone trips you up in the playgound at school, for no reason. You are badly hurt. Money falls out of your pocket and you lose it. You do not want to complain ot tell tales. Should you?

In the same incident, you eventually decide you must do something, and you complain to the teacher on playground duty. What should the teacher do?

In the same incident, what should you do, if the person you accuse (and whom you know to be the culprit) denies any knowledge of you or of what you are talking about?

The police catch you throwing a brick in the window of a tobacconists, late at night. You run away. A week later the policeman recognises you, but you deny having been anywhere near the shop. Does the policeman stand a good chance of securing your conviction if he takes you to court?

Three of you are friends, and go around as a gang. In a friendly fight, one of you goes too far and causes serious injury to someone else. Nobody knows (apart from the three of you) who is the particular one who did the action. All three are taken to the police station, and the police charge all three of you with the act in question. Would you continue to protect your friend?

In the same incident, the three of you are taken into separate rooms by the police for questioning. One of you (an innocent one) is told that the other two have ganged up on you, and have put the blame on you for what has happened. What would you do?

There is a gang of you, and you are about to attack a rival gang. The police come along, stop you, and arrest the lot of you. You complain that the police used violence in arresting you. The police answer that they had no option — you can only meet violence with violence. How might a magistrate resolve the dispute? Or a parent? Or a friend? Devise situations in which such an argument might take place.

* * *

How bad are teenage gangs?

Sometimes, though, the problem is not so much one of violence, as of the fear of violence. And nothing is quite so menacing, perhaps, as groups of young people 'hanging around' and 'up to no good':

Gang delinquency among the young has attracted publicity less because of its novelty than because of its drama. After all, bands of marauding youngsters were recorded in fourteenth century France. Shakespeare's 'Romeo and Juliet' shows the youthful members of rival families and their hangers-on roaming the streets and spoiling for a fight. In eighteenth century Brittany complaints were recorded of 'bold-faced adolescents, insolent, unbridled, mocking the laws of morality and humanity, taking pleasure in scandalising the respectable, infiltrating crowds and relieving them of their purses'. Nineteenth century cities, like New York and Paris, or London, Bristol or Glasgow could all produce accounts of groups of boys wandering the streets, living by pilfering from shops or stealing from passers-by. Dickens immortalised the Artful Dodger and his mates in 'Oliver Twist'. People like Mary Carpenter and Dr Barnardo tried to rescue them. Mayhew documented their background, careers and activities. . . .

There is always something very menacing in the ganging-up of young men against their elders or each other, a kind of primitive fear that encourages us to exaggerate the dangers they present, the harm they do. Recently in schools, on subways and on the streets, there have been nasty incidents of unprovoked violence. Police have had to be stationed in the corridors of many schools in New York. Yet it is easy to exaggerate the threat.

From *The Growth of Crime* by Leon Radzinowicz and Joan King
Hamish Hamilton 1977

For discussion
1 The article suggests that youthful violence has always been with us, and always will be. Would you agree?
2 The article also suggests that we can easily 'exaggerate the threat'. Would you agree? Why do you think we are inclined to exaggerate it?
3 Various theories have been put forward as to why some youths join 'violent' gangs. What might some of these theories be?

* * *

Violence and the police

The police have constantly to deal with violence of many different kinds, including violence to themselves. The following two cases occurred in Canada:

In February 1970, a civil servant named Walter Redel was on a sightseeing stroll through the city of Quebec when a car suddenly pulled up alongside him and two men jumped out. They stuck a gun in his ribs, told him they were policemen and tried to force him into their car. Redel could not be sure they were policemen, despite what they said, and resisted. They assaulted him so violently that when he was released (four hours later) from police custody he required three stitches above his left eye, four on the back of his head, and two on his lip. The police explanation was that Redel fitted the description of a wanted man, and had resisted arrest.

Question: should the police have used so much violence?
Second case:

In December 1968, two police officers at Minden, Ontario, volunteered to investigate a house disturbance caused by an armed man. Both officers had experience in handling mental patients with violent dispositions. They advanced towards the house, with outspread arms, to indicate that they were not armed. When they were within hearing distance, one of them called out, 'Put down your gun. . . Give us a chance to help.' The response was a burst of fire, killing both police officers.

Question: should the police in this situation have used more force?

Both cases are taken from *The Law and the Police* by Paula Bourne and John Eisenberg, copyright 1972 Ontario Institute for Studies in Education. Used by permission of Federal Publicity Co Limited, Don Mills, Ontario Canada.

These two cases illustrate the opposite sides of a basic dilemma — how to contain violence, how to stop it from spreading. Can you think of any situation in which you have seen *too much violence* used as a means of controlling violence? And can you think of any situation in which you have seen *too little violence* used for the same purpose?
What happened?
What would you do if these incidents occurred again and you were involved?

* * *

Invisible violence

So far we have been talking about violence in physical terms, and with some sort of bodily injury inflicted or anticipated. But of course we can talk of violence where the injury is not so much to the body as to the mind. Many psychologists would argue that very unhappy homes, for example, do more violence to a child's personality and welfare, than homes where, every now and again, people start hitting each other. The following are taken (and of course abbreviated) from some recent 'case histories':

1 A child's parents never spoke to each other, except through the child; even at mealtimes, they would appear not to hear each other, but only to hear the child's transmitted messages; instead of saying, Do you want the salt? they would say, Ask your father if he wants the salt. And so on. The child suffered serious strain and tension because of this.

2 A boy's father was very disappointed with his own career, and felt that he should have been much more successful than he was. He told the boy that he must do excellently at school, and the boy became petrified of failing to do so. In fact the boy did quite reasonably, and was a good average student. But he became seriously depressed because he was not outstanding.

3 A girl's mother constantly refused to let her have any opinion of her own. Whenever the girl's thoughts or feelings were in question, the mother would answer on her behalf. When the girl eventually tried to break away from her mother's influence, the mother told her she was a bad girl. The girl was so used to taking her mother's statements as her own, that she seriously believed she was bad and could see no point in living.

For discussion
1 Can the term 'violence' be applied to any or all these stories?
2 Take each of the stories in turn. Imagine that you are the *adult* in the story, and are being interviewed by the psychologist or social worker, after the child has broken down or been referred by the school. How might you explain what has happened?
3 Like most serious happenings, these stories are only slightly more intense versions of what happens some of the time to all of us. (Children are constantly ignored, etc.) Devise dramatic situations in which these same things happen but the child survives without injury. Improvise them.
4 Following 3, what happens to turn an ordinary case of family-conflict, into an extra-ordinary case of deep distress, breakdown, etc?
5 The Christian religion encourages us to turn the other cheek. Would this reduce the violence in our society? Have you ever yourself turned the other cheek? What happened?
   Devise a situation illustrating the Christian principle, and improvise it.

25 Espionage

(See also section 4 for the 'younger' group)

In fiction, mysteries are always solved. In life, they seldom are. A good example relates to the British spies Philby, Burgess and Maclean who during the '40s and early '50s, acted as Russian spies while employed by the British government in the diplomatic service or the secret service. How did they come to be recruited for the Russians? Was it a Russian working in Britain, or — more likely — was it an Englishman operating unsuspected on the Russians' behalf? If the latter, then it was very likely someone who knew them when they were young students at Cambridge University. And by a process of deduction we could then surmise that it was either a fellow student at Cambridge, or a teacher at the University.

> *Fourth man in Philby Case: University teacher suspected*
> The 25-year-old mystery of how Kim Philby, Donald Mclean and Guy Burgess were changed from undergraduate students into Russian spies in the 1930s, has never been resolved. But inquiries now under way, suggest that the missing fourth man was a wealthy Cambridge don.
> The don was a scholar of French literature, and his name was arrived at by a process of elimination. He would have been admirably placed to assist the three in disguising their treachery and planning their future careers. A large, jolly man, he was the best amateur actor of his generation and the life and soul of the university drama club.
> He was a great giver of parties, and was immensely popular. He would have known all three young men, and they would, no doubt, have trusted him as a man wiser and more experienced than themselves.
> The inquiries continue, but the suspect himself died in 1961.

In fact this particular news item proved false. The wealthy Cambridge don was revealed never to have been seriously considered as the missing 'fourth man'. Shortly after, other news items suggested other suspects. In the meantime, the mystery continues.

For discussion
1 Have you ever suspected someone who proved to be entirely innocent of the offence? What happened?
2 Have you ever come across a real-life mystery that remains unsolved? What happened?

3 By a process of elimination the detective can quite reasonably end up with the wrong man — as happened here. Devise a fictitious situation showing how this can happen. Improvise part of the story.

4 One of the reasons why we seldom catch the spy, is that we believe people most of the time to be honest, to be speaking the truth, to be what they appear to be.

A good example of the problem is given by Goronwy Rees in his book 'A Chapter of Accidents', in which he reveals that he knew Guy Burgess, and that Burgess confessed to him that he was a spy for the Russians. But Burgess and Rees were old friends, and Rees simply refused to believe him — and only remembered the incident years later when Burgess's guilt was all over the newspapers.

Devise a similar situation in which someone confesses to a crime, in circumstances where the other (very reasonably) cannot believe him. Improvise the scene.

* * *

Who spies?

What sort of people become spies? (Perhaps if we knew the answer to this question, we'd be able to stop espionage altogether.) Various German agents worked in the U.S.A. in the 1930s, and one of their great coups was to obtain highly secret information about the development of 'precision bombing'. *Hermann Lang* worked in a humble capacity at the plant where precision bombing techniques were perfected. *Frederick Duquesne* was a writer and 'professional' spy. Both lent their services to the Abwehr — the headquarters of German Intelligence activities. Both were Americans:

> Lang was a slight man in his mid-thirties, with dark blond hair and an open face that made one like and trust him at first blush. He was a machinist and draftsman, a naturalised American who had taken the oath of allegiance to the United Stated during his citizenship ceremony without concern. An unsophisticated working man, who had come to his moment of truth, he was elbowing his way into the most complex of games like a tinhorn who begins his gambling career by breaking the bank in Monte Carlo. He lived a regimented life with his wife and daughter in New York, and he was a good husband, a doting father and a fair provider. His wife and daughter would have been mortified had they known what he was up to.
>
> How does such a man become a spy? And why? Lang had a simple answer. He was not a Nazi, he was hazy about Hitler, and he had nothing against Hitler. But he considered himself a 'good German'. Yet it was not his ardent patriotism that propelled him into espionage. It was the opportunity that had come his way when he suddenly found

Who spies?

himself alone with those super-secret drawings.

And Duquesne:

> Duquesne was a professional spy, motivated by what he called his insatiable hatred of the British. A native of South Africa, he allegedly saw his mother tortured and killed in the Boer War and had sworn to avenge the 'dastardly deed'. He moved to England when the First World War broke out, volunteered his services to Germany as a secret agent, and embarked on his career in espionage. Some of his exploits — such as that he had guided the U-boat to the cruiser that was taking Lord Kitchener to Russia in 1917 and was thus responsible for Kitchener's death — were pure imagination. But he had done some genuine spying for the Germans and played a part in sabotaging ships and installations.
>
> After the war he took out American citizenship and established himself as a writer and lecturer. . . A deal was made, and Duquesne immediately went to work for the Abwehr.
>
> From *The Game of the Foxes* by Ladislas Farago, Hodder and Stoughton 1971

Of course, espionage still goes on. In 1977 two young Americans were found guilty of passing on secret information to the Russians. Christopher Boyce, aged 23, had a job handling secret information for a big defence manufacturer, TRW Systems Incorporated. He passed on the information to a friend, Andrew Lee, aged 25, who took it to a Russian agent in Mexico City:

> The operation began in 1975 and ended in January 1977 when Mr Lee, ignoring instructions from his Soviet contact, threw an envelope over the wall into the Soviet Embassy grounds in Mexico City and was spotted by Mexican police. Tiny strips of film negative, showing documents with 'Top Secret' written on them, were found on him, and he was sent to the United States for trial.
>
> One of the unanswered questions is what the motive of the two young spies could have been. They had grown up in a secluded area of expensive houses, and the two friends seemed to have everything that upper-middle-class America can bestow on young men. Mr Lee was perhaps in rebellion against his family: he was a bright student who dropped out after attending three different colleges in three years.

For discussion

1. Various reasons or motives are attributed in these stories to the different spies. What are they? Would you regard them as convincing reasons? What other reasons might there be?
2. The three British spies, Burgess, Philby and Mclean, all escaped to Russia before the British Government could bring charges against

them. How would you think such spies should be punished if found guilty?
3 Philby was quite definitely suspected of being a Russian Agent long before he fled to Russia, though he was compelled to resign from the British Secret Service before this. It has been suggested that the British authorities preferred to let him escape rather than be faced with a spy trial in order to find him officially 'guilty'. Why might this have been?
4 Can you think of any other situation in which it may be better to let a man escape, than to press formal charges against him? Can you think of any everyday situation in which people find it wiser to 'let someone get away with it'?
5 What would you do in the following cases:

You are the Chief of the Secret Service, or of an important branch of it. You are told privately that a key person in your service is providing information to the enemy. In fact, the only person who appears to have access to the information in question is yourself, but your private informant does not know this.

You are advised that three members of your service, all of whom defected to the Russian side, all studied at the same university at about the same time. How would you set about finding the 'contact' who possibly enrolled them on the enemy side?

You are advised that one of your team is possibly a double agent. There is no evidence as yet. How would you start sorting out the identity of the culprit?

You have a number of likely candidates for new members of the service. How would you go about choosing the best man?

Choose one of the situations from this set of questions, and use it as a basis for improvisation.

* * *

Structured improvisation

There are two characters: *Browne-Wilkinson,* the Head of the Secret Service and *Appleton,* a recent recruit to the service. Browne-Wilkinson has summoned Appleton for an urgent interview in his office. When Appleton arrives he is kept waiting for half an hour in the outer office. *Instructions for* APPLETON: you have the makings of a brilliant spy and will probably end up as the Chief of the Service. But you know you have to be extremely careful in every way, all of the time. You can't be *too* careful. For instance, a friend in the Service was telling you only this morning that 'they' (the Chief and Co) know *everything* about you, and although you cannot think off hand of anything you have done that you ought not to have done, you cannot be too sure of this. At the same time, you find it rather suspicious that so far you are not doing anything. You are being paid to sit around, as it were, reading the newspapers and 'getting to know the ropes'. In fact you spend most of your spare time going to the theatre (you did once belong to the dramatic society at college, and very nearly played in a production of 'Julius Ceasar' but were sacked because you could not remember your lines. This is something you never mention to anyone.) So you are determined to ask the chief for a proper assignment — something to do. But again, you have to be careful. Also, the Chief, you are told, is devious, and — who knows? — he might himself be a double agent. (Philby was, after all.) You find it especially worrying that after sending urgently for you, he should keep you waiting for half an hour. By the time you are invited into his room, you can only just conceal your anxiety and alarm.

Instructions for BROWNE-WILKINSON: you are a brilliant Chief, and enjoy your work immensely. You are at all times cool, suave, charming, and vaguely mysterious. Nobody quite knows what you are thinking, and you think this is just as it should be. Part of the reason for your success is that you have a good range of interests — you're not the sort of man who lives only for his work. You also run an amateur dramatic society, and you have discovered, looking through his file marked 'confidential' that Appleton was a brilliant amateur actor at university. So you have decided to ask Appleton to play in a forthcoming amateur production, directed by your wife, Emily, of Shakespeare's 'King Lear'. (You should decide, before the scene, the part you will want Appleton to play, and should bring along a copy of Shakespeare's play for Appleton to read an extract to you.) You're not entirely sure that Appleton will be right for the part, so you will want to audition him. Of course, this will mean that Appleton on no account must go out of town or out of the country while the production is in rehearsal. Now you are aware that Appleton may lack the good sense to realise that acting in plays is a good training for espionage, so you may possibly have to deceive him as to the justification of what you are getting him to do. (You might even go so far as hinting that foreign spies have infiltrated the dramatic society.) As regards the half hour delay while Appleton waits outside, this is to impress him and also to make him nervous. Now that you ask him in, at last, you will hint darkly that you have been engaged on important matters, perhaps on the phone to the Prime Minister, no less. Your intention is to impress him, manipulate him, and to get him firmly entrenched in Emily's forthcoming production.

26 Family Groups

Ask the class to look round at home and collect a set of old photographs. All the photos should be of groups of people, such as:
  a wedding photo
  a team of some kind
  a dramatic production, perhaps of a school play
  people in a street
  people on a ship, waving goodbye
  a family on holiday, perhaps on the beach
  a party of some kind
or they might be photos of old houses, farmsteads, etc.

In groups Choose the picture that seems the most interesting. Agree on a basic situation/background for the picture; if it is, for instance, a school play, say where the school is, what the play is, and when the photo was taken.

Individually Take a single character from the photo, or in the case of the house, of an individual who might live in the house or call at the house. Give your individual a biography; and then report back to the group with the details of the biography.

In groups Compare your various biographies, and to some extent make them 'consistent' with each other; ask questions of each other and expand the biographies as needs be. Prepare a production of a simple kind in which each of the characters can talk about himself/herself to the audience. This might be staged as the group in the photograph, with everyone still and silent except when it is his turn to soliloquise. Or it might be tape recorded. Or it might take the form of a photo-play, in which you play the recorded soliloquys while showing a set of photos of the characters and perhaps the setting. (And there are of course many other possibilities.) NB The soliloquys could be in prose, or verse. You might also like to experiment with the use of music in the background, in order to set and vary the mood and atmosphere.

You might also like to incorporate snatches of dialogue, and perhaps of extracts from news stories of the time, and perhaps of extracts from contemporary literature. Since your aim is to build up a portrait of a group of people in 'time past' and 'time remembered' you will look around for the various ways in which you might do this.

27 Crime and Punishment

Tom Hart was a housemaster in a children's home when he first met Alan, then a 7-year-old already being shunted from one institution to another. He later got caught up in petty crime and drug addiction, and finally killed himself (aged 30) in Wandsworth Prison. Tom Hart knew Alan on and off throughout his life:

> On various occasions I talked to Alan about prison and prisoners. Being in prison, he would say, the actual prison itself was not unduly hard; the food was not particularly good, but that you could live on it and prison officers did not go out of their way to make trouble for the prisoners. . .
> The prison routine was monotonous, even, in his view, for those who participated willingly, and it was even more monotonous for those in prison who were not very bright. He said that some of them had been in and out of prison so often that they did not know how to cope unless they were inside, and, he said, 'I hope to God I never get that way' — and yet, in his frightened, half-formed knowledge of himself, he had begun to see his future as 'in and out of prison'. He said the problem with prisons was that there was no one day that was different from any other, that you went on living the same day, no matter how long you were there — in for three years, it was one day of three years, and you lived in a fantasy world, along with other men, discussing what you would do when you got out. Some men believed the police were idiots, and that they had been caught because of bad luck and imagined that next time they would have learnt by their mistake.
> 'As you listen you realise just how hopeless their future is, and after a time you appreciate you can't isolate yourself from them and you begin to indulge in fantasies too, about how things will be better and what you will do to ensure that you do not return.'
>
> Prison, he said, had its own smell, and any man who has spent time in prison, as 'screw' or convict, would still recognise that smell when he was ninety years old. It was the smell of dust, grease and stale urine. He said that when slopping-out time came he could only imagine what it was like to live in a sewer. It was the slopping out, he said, that stripped a man of his pride and dignity, and that was the one advantage a prison officer had over the prisoners — he didn't have to do it.

He said that the prison officer, unless a remarkable man, could only end up in time very like the prisoners, completely demoralised with little idea of the world outside.

From *A Walk with Alan* by Tom Hart, Quartet Books 1973

For discussion

1 How do you feel about Alan's comments on prison life? Do you find them plausible?
2 What is the most striking part of Alan's comments? What seems to him to be the greatest punishment in being imprisoned?
3 Alan feels as sorry for the prison officer as for the prisoner. How might the officer see his own role? What would he see as the purpose of his work?
4 What do you think are the aims of punishment? What does the law seek to do when it builds prisons?
Note down these different aims. How far does imprisonment fulfil the aims?
5 One of the aims of punishment is that it should prevent crime, or at least reduce the crime rate. But not only do police reports indicate that the crime rate never gets reduced, but also there is evidence to suggest that most criminals are never caught, and that most of us are criminals:

> On the basis of their own admissions, it appears that very few people, less than one in ten, have never been guilty of lawbreaking at all . . . Crimes fully brought into the open and punished represent no more than 15 per cent of the great mass actually committed.
>
> From *The Growth of Crime* by Leon Radzinowicz and Joan King

From your own experience, does this statement seem credible? — or exaggerated?
Is there a solution to this problem?
Is it a problem? (ie should we worry that many crimes go undetected?)
Devise a situation illustrating the 'problem'. (The setting might be a store, for example, or a school.) Improvise it.
6 Another aim of punishment is, usually, that it should in some way fit the crime. The following is an example of a very definite attempt to do this:

> Three boys aged 11, 12 and 13, yesterday reported for three hours of work at a wild fowl refuge at Snettisham, Norfolk, by order of a magistrate. They will have to return on three more weekends.
>
> 'The punishment to fit the crime' order was made at Hunstanton

Juvenile Court. The offence: taking four eggs and destroying a swan's nest. The boys were put on probation for a year on condition that they put in four periods of three hours at the refuge.

How might other punishments be designed to fit the crime? In general is this a desirable aim? Is it attainable? The Old Testament advocates 'an eye for an eye, a tooth for a tooth'. Is this the same thing as punishment fitting the crime? Do you agree with the Old Testament rule?

7 Many people believe that punishments are simply not heavy enough:

'I favour the reintroduction of capital punishment for murder. I believe that we would save innocent lives. There is ample evidence that the present life sentence for murder is not proving an effective deterrent.'
Mr William Walker, prospective parliamentary candidate for Perth, said that for too long, 'the reformers and softies' had been allowed to influence the ways teenage thugs were handled. He suggested the introduction of 12 months' compulsory national service for all young people over 18 and under 25 who had been more than three months away from full-time education or gainful employment.

What do you think about Mr Walker's views? Imagine that you are Mr Walker, and that you are being questioned (by the whole class) on the rest of your views and attitudes, perhaps immediately prior to the parliamentary election. Improvise the interview. (Extend the subject-matter beyond the law and order issue into national and international affairs.)

8 A recent report by the National Association for the Care and Resettlement of Offenders recommended that the vast majority of juvenile offenders should *not* be put inside residential institutions, such as Borstal, but should be looked after in the community itself. (Among other things, they could be placed with foster-parents.)

What are the advantages and disadvantages of this proposal? If you yourself became involved in a criminal offence, what would be your own preference?

9 All of us break the law at some time, and all of us at some time get punished for doing so. Mostly the law in question is not the law of the state but the law of the home, of parents, of school etc. In general, what kinds of punishment do you think effective? Illustrate from your own experience. And what kinds do you find ineffective or counter-productive? Take an example and improvise it.

10 Consider the following cases, in all of which the prisoner has been found guilty as charged. What kinds of punishment would you recommend:

(a) an old man has been convicted many times of various charges of petty theft, and has spent over thirty years in prison. He steals a cake from a cake-shop.
(b) the same old man, instead of stealing from a shop, breaks into a house by a back door, and steals a cake from a larder. While making his getaway an old lady living in the house walks into the kitchen, sees him, and is so frightened that she has a heart-attack and dies.
(c) a young man, with no criminal record of any kind, loses his temper with a boy who pushes in front of him in a bus queue. He hits him so hard the boy is taken to hospital and is unable to walk again for a month. The young man is genuinely ashamed of what he has done.
(d) two girls, aged 17, kidnap a baby. They do it for fun, to see if they can get away with it. They make a ransom demand and are caught by the police. The baby is unharmed.
(e) the same two girls, but this time the baby dies through neglect. The girls show no regret and tell the police the whole thing is very amusing.
(f) a boy has recently left school and can find no work. He goes housebreaking, and is found by an elderly man rummaging through his kitchen. The man attacks the boy with a bread knife and in the struggle, the man is seriously wounded.
(g) the same boy, the same old man, but the old man eventually dies in hospital.
(h) in a family row, a girl runs away from home and breaks into a friend's house and steals money.
(i) the same girl, after conviction and punishment for the above offence, runs away again, stealing this time from her parents. She tells the police she will not live at home again.

Imagine that you are a social worker/probation officer etc., and that you are asked to interview the accused in any of the above cases and to advise the court before sentence is imposed. Improvise the interview.

28 Folies à Deux

Friendship of any kind is based, in part, on shared interests, attitudes and beliefs. Sometimes a friendship is based on a shared *delusion*, in which the friends act upon the belief that something exists that does not exist. In one sense this is true of most friendships and most close relationships. But at its most intense this shared delusion can become a shared mental sickness, known to psychologists as a *folie à deux*.

An example of a *folie à deux* occurs in the play 'Who's Afraid of Virginia Woolf?' by Edward Albee, in which a childless married couple console themselves by 'inventing' and talking a great deal about a child whom others quite naturally believe to exist. And in Harold Pinter's play 'Old Times' a married couple invent a third person who is the old friend of the wife and the old flame of the husband. (Or at least this is one possible interpretation of the enigmatic outsider in this play!)

Sometimes the *folie* can produce very serious, indeed deadly, results, as in the following two news stories:

1   ...The couple murdered the child in the sincere belief that he was possessed by the devil, and that there was no other way of ridding the house of the devil's influence. The defence lawyer further pleaded that the wife acted entirely under the influence of the husband, and that it was he who first 'saw' and then 'showed' to the wife, the presence of the devil in the body of the son. . . . .

2   *Woman kept in filthy cellar for 37 years*
Signora Giovanna Lucia Tiana, aged 73, has been brought out of a cellar in the Sardinian village of Bultei, in which she has spent the last 37 years of her life without light, amid rats and filth.
Police who released her during the weekend were reported as saying that when they found her, the scene was such that they would never want to see its like again.
The woman had been imprisoned in the cellar by her two brothers because they said she was possessed by the devil. They were both arrested.

For discussion
1 How do such delusions grow up? How do people come to share them?

2 Have you ever come across any similar incidents? What happened?
3 Most friendships are based on some kind of *'folie à deux'* — a shared belief in the existence of something that to other people's thinking does not exist. Would you agree? Can you give an instance of this from your own lives?
4 "Small children create numerous *folies* and take great pleasure in sharing them with one another. But they seldom share them with an adult." Would you agree with this? Can you remember such a thing from your own childhood?

* * *

Not all *folies à deux* end up with murder. The psychiatrist *Charles Rycroft* gives an example in which a patient of his developed acute anxieties for the safety of the country and of himself. He became convinced that enemy forces were digging a tunnel from overseas and heading in the direction of his own neighbourhood. To meet the impending crisis, (which everyone else seemed to ignore) he proceeded to build his own hydrogen bomb:

> It would be capable of destroying the whole world. . . (but) was a pathetic contraption, improvised out of lead piping, ball-bearings and wire, and only in its creator's imagination could it be conceived to have any function at all.

Now the patient, a young man, eventually showed the bomb to his landlady and she:

> . . . watched its growth with the sympathetic indulgence that she would have given to something a child of her own was making out of Meccano. . . . His landlady tolerated his eccentric behaviour, enjoying his dependence on her, and protected him from external reality.

In other words, she entered into the young man's fantasy, and at least acted as if she believed it. They shared his delusion of an impending disaster and of the importance of the young man's bomb. They were happy in their shared, fool's paradise. Rycroft suggests that the reason for this was the landlady's own loneliness and her regrets that she did not have a child of her own:

> . . .she regarded him solely as a child and not at all as a childish adult. . . My patient and she colluded to form a *folie à deux* by which he was able to act out his fantasies, and she found an outlet for unsatisfied maternal impulses.

But such things cannot last forever (presumably):

> At the end of July his young brother arrived in England, and he seemed quite incapable of accepting how ill the patient was and my advice that he should handle him gently. Instead he treated him as though he were not ill at all, and made no attempt to conceal his contempt for his brother's contraption (the bomb). As a result Mr Y found that his bomb, which had previously been the subject of interpretation by myself and of indulgent interest by his landlady, had suddenly become an object of mockery, and that he himself had become the butt of his brother's sarcastic humour.
>
> His reaction to the situation was increasing tension and violence, and eventually he had to be committed to hospital.
>
> Adapted from *Imagination and Reality* by Charles Rycroft, Hogarth Press 1968

For discussion
1 What should the landlady have done, or should she have behaved as she did?
2 The young man's story is an extreme example of something we all do, in one way or another: indulge in delusions, and convince ourselves of their reality. Have you ever done this? What happened?
Has any one ever tried (successfully or otherwise) to *share* a delusion with you? Can you think of cases where this has happened to other people? (You can perhaps draw examples from fiction as well as reality.)
3 The brother could not accept that the young man was ill, and so he was largely instrumental in causing his breakdown. Why are we so reluctant to believe such things?
4 Which of the characters, if any, would you blame for the breakdown? — the man himself, the psychiatrist (who knew what was happening but was trying to treat the patient) the landlady, the brother?
5 Devise a situation in which two people share what is perhaps a delusion, and a third person gets involved with them. Improvise the story.

* * *

Structured improvisation
There are two characters, an old age pensioner and a policewoman. The pensioner has phoned the police earlier in the day from a public call-box and has asked for police protection. He claims to have been assualted by a neighbour. The police officer arrives to see the pensioner three hours later.

The pensioner (Mr Crawford) has neighbours on both sides: the Macmurrays and the Robertsons. The Macmurrays have moved in recently, and the Robertsons have lived there many years, as has Crawford.

Instructions for CRAWFORD: you have been widowed for three years, and both your children have grown up and you never see them from one year's end to another. Your wife was a wonderful woman, and there is no one like her. Your two children would come to see you, but they both have very important jobs and cannot afford the time. You know they would come if you ever asked them to, but you are independent and you trouble no one. The country is going to the dogs, everything is deteriorating, and nobody does anything to stop the rot. Take your new neighbours: a terrible lot (the Macmurrays). He never does any work, lives on the social security (you see him going to the security offices every week, large as life) and almost certainly is a crook of some kind. The most disreputable and shady characters are forever calling there with strange packages under their arms. Of course other people's business is their own business, and you never spy on them. But recent developments have caused you a great deal of concern. The Macmurrays have started banging on the wall in the middle of the night. Who, knows, perhaps they are building cupboards to hide stolen goods? You were kept awake night after night until you decided, last night, to charge round to them (in the middle of the night) and demand an explanation. Macmurray eventually came to the door, in his pyjamas, and when he refused to stop the noise, you told him exactly what you thought of him and his wife. The upshot was that he punched you on the nose. You went straight to the phone box for police protection. It has taken them three hours to arrive, and from the front room window (looking from behind the curtain) you have seen the police officer call first on the neighbours on both sides.

NB: you enjoy talking, and you have much to tell the police officer (in addition to the complaint about the assault) about the decline of the nation and the neighbourhood and the neighbours. Your important aim is to persuade the police to take the Macmurrays to court and charge them with something.

Instructions for THE POLICE OFFICER: you have been advised by your superior officer that Crawford is a slightly mad, and very troublesome old man, who frequently complains about everyone, and especially about his neighbours. Your task therefore is really just to humour him. You called in first on the Macmurrays, and they seem to you a very decent, law-abiding family. Mr Macmurray said he had never seen Mr Crawford, but Mrs Macmurray though she had seen him last night (from her bedroom window) running up the footpath in front of his house and shouting. She took no notice. You gather that Macmurray does not go out to work, but lives — so he says, at least — on an inheritance from his wife's parents, who won the Irish Sweepstake many years ago.

You called on the Robertsons, who are quite elderly. They say that Crawford is a great nuisance, and keeps on disturbing them. He makes a lot of knocking and banging noises in the middle of the night and they have several times had to complain — without any success. Last night, they tell you, the noises were particularly disturbing, and Mr Robertson went round and knocked on Crawford's street door in the early hours of the morning. There was no response, and eventually he went back to bed and forgot all about it. You now call on Crawford, to get his story. You may well decide to make notes so that you have the full details for reporting back to your superiors.

29 Fraudulent Conversion

A mock trial, devised as a structured improvisation. These preliminary notes should be discussed, first, with the whole class: individual instructions could perhaps be given by photo-copy.

The Procedure in Court
The case takes place in the Court of Quarter Sessions, which is presided over by a Recorder. The Recorder is a practising barrister of some distinction, and his work as Recorder occupies only a part of his time. The rest of the time he will probably himself be fighting cases in higher courts. The Recorder is the chairman of the court, and the judge. All remarks must be addressed to him, except where the barristers are directly addressing the jury or a witness. The Recorder's task is to see that the case is fairly conducted, that no irrelevant evidence is brought forward, and to sum up the evidence to the jury. If a prisoner is found guilty, then the Recorder must also deliver sentence.

The sequence of the case is as follows:
1. The prisoner is charged by the clerk of the court, and the prisoner pleads guilty or not guilty.
2. The prosecution outlines the facts of the case as revealed by the prosecution evidence given in the magistrates' court.
3. The prosecution calls its witnesses and obtains from them, by simple and direct questions, all the relevant evidence from which it is possible to deduce the guilt of the accused. There must be no leading questions –ie, questions which imply the answer. An example would be, 'Is it not correct that the person you saw walking away in the fog was walking with a slight limp in the right leg, similar to the prisoner's?' At the same time though, it is permissible to ask leading questions if they are merely going over ground about which there is no dispute.
4. Once the prosecution has finished examining a particular witness – and this must be done very thoroughly and no details, however trivial, must be left out – then the defence counsel has the right to cross-examine the witness on the evidence he has just given. The prosecution then has the right to re-examine the witness, in order to clear up any points raised in the cross-examination.
5. When all the prosecution witnesses have given their evidence, the defence opens its case. Counsel briefly explains that it intends to

Fraudulent Conversion

prove the accused's innocence, and then proceeds to call the defence witnesses — usually including the accused himself. These witnesses are cross-examined and re-examined just as the prosecution witnesses were.

6 Defence sums up its case and urges the jury to return a verdict of not guilty.
7 Prosecution sums up its case and urges the jury to return a verdict of guilty.
8 The Recorder sums up the whole trial, reviewing the evidence in great detail and carefully considering it, but without attempting to tell the jury what their decision should be. He points out any inconsistencies or unexplained details.
9 The jury retires and, under the chairmanship of the foreman of the jury, considers its verdict. There are usually twelve jurors: provided only two jurors disagree with the remainder, their verdict does not, since the Criminal Justice Act 1967, have to be unanimous.
10 The jury returns, the clerk of the court asks the foreman to pronounce the verdict, the prisoner standing at this time, and the verdict is announced. The Recorder then either acquits the prisoner if the verdict is 'not guilty', or proceeds to deliver sentence.

Before the Trial

Defence counsel interviews the prisoner, in order to obtain in detail his version of the facts. This interview must of course be done in the absence of all the other characters. In an actual case it might take place in a special room in the court house, perhaps only shortly before the case is heard. Quite often the barrister does not himself interview the prisoner at all — this is done by a solicitor who then prepares a dossier/brief which is given to the barrister.

R v. Woodrow (adapted from the author's book, *Talking* Batsford 1968
Characters
    The Recorder
    Counsel for the Defence
    Counsel for the Prosecution
    The Jury (This could be the rest of the class.)

Witnesses for the Defence:
    COLIN WOODROW, the accused. Bookmaker's clerk., aged 26. Treasurer of the Old Redbridgeans Cricket Club.
    DOUGLAS HAMPTON, aged 28. School teacher. Committee member of the Club. Knew the accused at school. Now teaches at his old school.

Witnesses for the Prosecution:
    TOM BANFORTH, aged 64. Bank manager. Married. Chairman of Club.

HENRY DEWEY, aged 26. Knew accused at school. Reporter on local newspaper. Secretary of the Club.

GEORGE FIELD, aged 50. Floor manager at departmental store. Married. One son at art college. Committee member of the Club.

The Charge

Woodrow is charged with the fraudulent conversion of £500.

Fraudulent conversion is an offence punishable with imprisonment for a period not exceeding seven years. It is committed when a person fraudulently converts to his own use property with which he had been entrusted for safe-keeping.

Instructions for ALL THREE CHARACTERS: five weeks ago, Colin Woodrow, aged 26, was charged at the Magistrates' Court with the fraudulent conversion of £500 — being a sum of money entrusted to him in his capacity as Honorary Treasurer of the Old Redbridgeans Cricket Club. Woodrow pleaded not guilty, reserved his defence and elected to go to the Quarter Sessions for trial by jury. The evidence as revealed by the prosecution witnesses at the Magistrates' Court was as follows:

From the ages of 11 to 18, Colin Woodrow was a pupil at the Redbridge High School. He left the school with two 'A' levels, and took up work as an articled clerk to a solicitor, which meant five years of training and examinations, at the end of which time he would, if successful at his exams, become a fully qualified solicitor. On leaving school he joined the Old Redbridgeans Society, and played for the Old Boys' rugby and tennis clubs. When he first became an Old Boy there was no cricket club attached to the Old Boys' Association. Interest in the game among Old Boys had apparently dropped off in the previous years, partly, it was felt, because the Old Boys owned no kind of club house which was near to the local cricket grounds. The rugby club own a club house which is just opposite their rugby pitch, and the tennis club own the house and grounds where they play tennis. Woodrow had been a keen cricketer at school, and was anxious to continue playing. He invited other Old Boys who were interested to contact him, and to set up a new club, designed to encourage the playing of cricket, and to attract funds with which to purchase a cricket club house. As a result of his endeavours, the Old Boys' Society, at an Annual General Meeting, elected a cricket club committee, consisting of: Tom Banforth (Chairman), Henry Dewey (Secretary), Douglas Hampton, George Field and Colin Woodrow (Treasurer).

When the Committee was first elected a year ago, it was given the job of persuading members to join the Cricket Club and acquiring funds for the eventual purchase of a club house. It is agreed that no conditions were laid down as to how the treasurer should look after the money that was so collected. It is also agreed that since its formation the committee

Fraudulent Conversion

has met at the home of the chairman the first Monday (evening) of each month to discuss policy. The committee first of all applied for the names of Old Boys who wanted to join the cricket club and who were anxious to assist in the purchase of a club house. Only thirty Old Boys applied, and at a special meeting for all those who were interested, it was unanimously agreed that they would all, including members of the committee, pay to the Treasurer the sum of £1, to represent one year's subscription, and to provide the club with some small sum of money from which to start campaigning for more. A series of dances were held in a local dance hall, and as a result of admission charges and raffles, a further £250 was collected for the club funds. All this money was deposited with the accused, the treasurer. Other clubs within the Old Boys' Association were then approached for small donations, as a result of which the club received further gifts bringing the whole sum of money deposited with the accused to a total of £500.

This was the financial position four months ago.

Four months ago, at a committee meeting, the Treasurer made his monthly statement of account to the committee. Since the money had now reached a considerable sum, the Chairman, Banforth, proposed that it was now high time that the committee opened a bank account in the name of the club. Up to that time the accused had been keeping the money in his own account. This motion was passed unanimously and the accused promised to arrange matters accordingly. It was agreed that the most sensible thing was to open an account at the Chairman's own bank. (The accused banks elsewhere.) At the same time it was agreed that the club had already made sufficient progress to warrant arranging cricket matches for the next season. At this same meeting, Henry Dewey, the secretary of the club, raised the question of investing the £500 in a club house as soon as possible. It was agreed that the treasurer would look into the question of mortgage arrangements and that all the committee members would keep a lookout for likely properties.

Two months ago, the chairman came to the monthly meeting with the announcement that he had seen an ideal club house, situated near to the cricket pitch, and which it was fairly certain they could acquire with a deposit of £500. He asked the accused why he had not yet arranged for the money to be deposited in a separate account, and the accused explained that he was in process of doing so. The chairman obtained the approval of the committee − by a unanimous vote − to investigate the purchase of the proposed property. Two weeks later, he phoned the accused to say that the legal papers were all ready, that they could go ahead, and that all that was needed was for the accused to pay over the money for the deposit on the property. The accused then revealed that he no longer had the money, and that he had himself used the money as a bet on a horse race, and had lost it entirely and was unable at that time to repay it.

The chairman contacted the police.

When charged by the police with fraudulent conversion, the accused pleaded that the committee had told him to place the money on the bet, and that he never intended at any time to use the money for his own purposes, or to use the winnings for the bet if he had in fact backed a winner. The bet was placed on the authority of the committee, and if the bet had been a good one then the club would have made enough money — £15 000 — to pay the purchase money for the club house outright. Hence, says the accused, he had no intention to commit any crime.

The details of Woodrow's career since becoming an articled clerk to a solicitor were summarised to the Magistrates' Court as follows:

After three years of working with the solicitor, the accused, who was then aged 21, left this employment and worked in various odd jobs — including some clerical and some labouring jobs — and then, a year ago, at the age of 25, became a chief clerk to a leading firm of bookmakers who have a large office in the town. He still works there.

The accused has no previous convictions.

Instructions for THE INDIVIDUAL CHARACTERS

Witnesses for the Prosecution
TOM BANFORTH, aged 64. A bank clerk in the town for many years, and now a bank manager. Joined the Old Redbridgeans when you first left school and have been active in it ever since. You used to serve on many committees within the Society, and were at one time President of the Society.

You have been in the bank all your working life except for the War, when you served in the Service Corps, and rose to the rank of Captain. You are intensely proud of your old school tie and were a promising scholar when you were at school. You had the chance of going on to university, but in those days scholarships and grants were hard to come by, and your parents needed you to add to the weekly wage packet. You were slightly resentful of the enormous opportunities afforded to modern youth but have no grudge against anyone, and are an absolutely fair man. There are, however, certain things of which you strongly disapprove. To be precise, there are three: gambling, drinking and not going to church. You are a staunch churchgoer, and are in fact a churchwarden. You have never in your life consumed any intoxicating liquor of any form. You have never gambled. You watched with strong distaste when during the 1950s the laws were changed and gambling shops were allowed to open, and indeed did open in vast quantities. You consider this a sign of, and a cause of, the slow decline which you believe to be taking place in the moral standards of this country.

Your wife shares these views with you. She too, is a keen churchgoer.

Fraudulent Conversion

You had one son, who was killed in an air raid, when he was 2 years old.

The Old Boys' Society is one of your prime joys in life. You go along to the school itself as often as you are invited — and never miss a prize day.

When you heard that someone was hoping to form an Old Boys' Cricket Club you were immediately interested, and have always regretted the fact that the original cricket club for some reason has faded out. You were elected as chairman of the committee set up to help re-form the cricket club, and you were generally impressed by the calibre of the other men on the committee. Dewey seems a likeable young man, though slightly excitable and over-enthusiastic, but then newspaper reporters are never the most stable of people. At least Dewey is not apparently a great drinker, as you believe so many reporters to be. You have stressed from the beginning that if a club house is eventually acquired, it is not to be used for the purpose of drunken gatherings. Drinking, if there must be drinking, must be kept down to modest quantities.

Hampton also seems pleasant enough. He is not as formidable as teachers used to be, and ought to be, but for all that not a bad fellow, you suppose. Field seems to be something of a hanger on, and indeed almost a joke. He has managed to worm his way into every committee in existence — at least within the Old Boys' Association. Field has the depressing habit of wanting to please everyone, and to agree with everyone. But he seems honest enough for all that.

When you discovered that young Woodrow was a bookmaker's clerk, you were naturally somewhat irritated. Even more so, when he started to talk about gambling at the committee meetings. But you soon stopped that, by simply ruling it out of order. The committee meetings have been held every month in your own home, and you have controlled and dominated them all quite effectively. The steps leading up to the intended purchase of a club house were all handled by yourself and but for this most unfortunate and embarrassing business with Woodrow spending all the money for his own purposes, on a racing bet at that, the club house would now be a reality.

You do not feel at all vindictive towards Woodrow, and have no doubt that if his gamble had paid off, he would have kept the profit for himself and returned the £500 to the club.

You cannot imagine how he can dare to plead that the bet was placed with the consent of the committee.

HENRY DEWEY, aged 26. A local newspaper reporter. You knew the accused at school and were for a time in the same class as he was. Did not like him particularly at that time, and were even slightly envious of the fact that he appeared to be rather better at school work than you were, and that he went up into the sixth form, while you left school aged 16. Have worked on the same newspaper ever since, learning the job in all its aspects. You have played rugby for the Old Boys since leaving school, and became interested in the idea of a cricket club as soon as you heard about the proposal a year or so ago.

Two months ago, the chairman, Banforth, whom you regard as something of an old stick-in-the-mud, raised the question of purchasing a £15 000 club house. At that time, the accused, as treasurer, was holding £500 on behalf of the club. After the meeting, which was of course held at the chairman's house, the accused invited yourself and George Field to the local pub for a quick drink. In the course of the drink, he suggested to the two of you, that if you agreed to the proposal, then he would invest the £500 on a very sound bet, so as to multiply the sum of money that the club possessed, and to give them the chance of purchasing much more spacious accommodation than that proposed by Banforth. Field said that he thought this was a bad idea, unless the chiarman were to be persuaded to agree with it. The accused pointed out that Banforth was opposed to almost everything, and particularly to gambling. Field then appeared to agree to the proposal. You took the line that the porposed club house was not a very good one, and if the idea of a bet could be made to work, then so much the better. The following week, the accused phoned you up. He told you that he knew of the most safe bet imaginable and that the odds were ten to one. You replied that if he was absolutely certain then he should go ahead, but that if the bet failed, then he would have to take the responsibility. The accused agreed to this, and said there was no risk of losing the money — it was the safest bet imaginable.

The next thing you heard was a week later when the accused phoned you to say that he had lost the money, that he had been accused by the chairman of using the money for his own purposes, and that he was likely to be prosecuted in the courts. You replied that you had no idea what he was talking about.

Your own attitude is quite right and proper: you warned Woodrow that if he took a gamble it would be his own responsibility, and you have no intention of involving yourself in any way in the liability either for the crime or for the lost money. Woodrow admittedly spoke to you privately before making the bet, and it seems clear in your own mind that it was never his intention to walk off with the money made from the bet. But at the same time, you cannot see how you can explain all this to the court without in some way or other involving yourself in the case and the charge. And you are merely doing what you originally told Woodrow you would do — having nothing to do with his project if it failed.

There remains only the question of George Field, who was with Woodrow and yourself in the pub at the time when the idea was first put forward by the accused. You phoned up Field before the case was heard in the Magistrates' Court and you asked him what he intended to reveal. To your delight, you discovered that he intended to reveal nothing.

Unfortunately you completely forgot to decide with him whether you both intend to agree that you went with the accused to the pub on the night in question. Your own thought on the subject is that the best thing to say is that you did indeed go, and that the accused did invite you, but that you did not discuss any question of a bet. Unfortunately you forgot to raise this point with Field, and it does not cross your mind until you are sitting waiting to give evidence, by which time, of course it is too late. You hope that Field will have the common sense not to deny the meeting in the pub. After all, the pub was crowded, and although nobody overheard what was said, many people must have seen and recognised the three of you.

GEORGE FIELD, aged 50. Married with one son, who is now a student at an art college. Extremely pleasant and friendly personality. Active in the Old Boys' Association for many years. Very fond of Mr Banforth, who is sometimes rather puritanical and testy, but a good sort for all that — one of the best. Spent all working life since leaving school at the local department store, where you are now a floor manager. Your health has been shaky for some time now, and you are particularly troubled with arthritis. This often makes walking and standing about very painful. Your employers, have several times suggested that you should find employment of a different kind, involving no standing or walking, but you are well aware that at your age it is virtually impossible to find fresh employment. Besides, your son is still at college, and he may yet want financial assistance from you, and so it would be fatal to switch jobs at this stage. The present case has caused you a great deal of distress. When Banforth first raised the question of purchasing a club house at the meeting two months ago, Dewey and yourself were invited out for a drink afterwards by the accused, Woodrow. At this friendly drinking session, Woodrow, who is of course a bookmaker's clerk, proposed that he should invest the £500 that he was holding for the club, on a safe bet, and that the club would then be able to buy a much better club house. To your later regret, you agreed to this proposal, on the grounds that Woodrow was a very bright young man, not unlike your own son, and that since he was in the betting business, he was sure to know a safe bet when he saw one. When you heard of the loss of the money, you thought at first of confessing that the accused had asked your permission. But then, young Dewey phoned you up and intimated that he intended to deny knowing anything about it. As he pointed out, if you said you knew about it, the tables could easily be turned and you could be accused of intending to use the money for your own purposes. Regretfully, you decided to deny all knowledge of the matter.

Witnesses for the Defence
DOUGLAS HAMPTON, aged 29. Educated at Redbridge, won State Scholarship to King's College, London. Graduated in History, returned to Red-

bridge as assistant history master. Joined Old Boys' Association, and was very interested in proposed cricket club. Elected to committee. You knew the accused as a schoolboy and got along well with him. Were surprised to hear that he had left the solicitors' profession, but you don't doubt that he will make a very prosperous and successful bookmaker.

You found the monthly meetings very dull, especially as the chairman, Banforth, did most of the talking, and he is a notorious old bore.

You first suspected that the accused was not keeping strictly to his treasurer's role some four months ago when Banforth pointed out at a meeting that the accused had not yet invested the club's money in a separate account, and that he should do so immediately. You were intrigued to note that a month or so later Woodrow had still not taken the money out of his own private account. It seemed not impossible to you that Woodrow had got involved in some kind of financial troubles and that he had used the club money to pay off his debts. You were made more suspicious when you noted that Woodrow made a particular point, after a meeting two months ago, the last meeting prior to the flaring up of the case, of inviting Field and Dewey out for a drink. It almost looked as though a plot was being laid. And while you know Field is a pleasant and quite harmless old boy, you are less sure of Dewey, whom you vaguely remember from your schooldays along with Woodrow himself. Were they both in the same class? You have a feeling they were.

About a week later you decided that it was quite possible that Woodrow had got himself into some kind of a mess, and so you phoned Woodrow and decided to ask him categorically what was happening to the £500. To your surprise Woodrow told you that the previous day he had placed the money (£500) on a bet, and that the odds had been ten to one. It had apparently been a safe bet, but it had failed and the money was now lost. Woodrow explained that he would eventually be able to replace the lost money. The only risk was that Banforth would want to see the money before Woodrow had a chance to replace it. When you told Woodrow that he had behaved most foolishly he replied that he had consulted Field and Dewey and gained their approval, and that he would have consulted you also, but you seemed the sort of person who would have disapproved of the idea, as indeed you would have done. When the police charged Woodrow with fraudulent conversion, you telephoned him to say that you would be willing to testify on his behalf in court. He then told you that both Field and Dewey had denied having any prior knowledge of the bet.

COLIN WOODROW: you have had great success as a bookmaker's clerk. Provided this case does not land you in prison, you should do well, and will probably get your own business before long. You never for one moment intended to convert the £500 to your own use, nor to use even the profits on the bet for your own use. The position was very simple:

you know a good bet when you see one, and you knew full well that if you could hold on to the club money you would eventually be able to place it on a safe bet and multiply it overnight. You very much wanted to do this. Not for any personal glory, but just because the opportunity existed, and it seemed wicked to waste it. This was why you played for time when old Banforth suggested that you place the money in a separate account. You knew of course that Banforth would never agree to using the money on a gamble. He was famous for his opposition to gambling and also to drinking. But you felt happier about Dewey, whom you were with at school, and old Field, who is a friendly and easy type. So, after the committee meeting two months ago, you quietly approached Field and Dewey, invited them round to the local for a drink, and suggested to them that you should invest the money on a good gamble. Field and Dewey, after some initial persuasion, agreed to this. You thought about approaching the remaining member of the committee, Douglas Hampton, the young school teacher, but eventually thought better of it. After all, he would be unlikely to understand the gambler's instincts.

Before actually placing the bet you phoned Dewey to get his assurance that he approved of your plan. This was a week after the meeting in the pub. Dewey was not encouraging. He made it clear that if the bet went wrong, then you would have to accept the responsibility on your own. You took this to mean that he would not pay for any of the lost money, and since you never intended that he should do so, you decided to go ahead and place the bet. It was, of course, a disaster.

The following day you were telephoned by Hampton, the teacher, who had apparently suspected that something was wrong, to ask where the money was. You told him the whole story. You added that everything would be all right provided Banforth did not suddenly demand to see the money before you had the chance to replace it. Hampton told you that you had behaved most foolishly. A few days later the inevitable happened. Banforth phoned you up, demanded to see the money and you had to reveal the whole story. When you telephoned Dewey, he declared that he did not know what you were talking about, and you then phoned Field also, who responded in the same fashion. You then phoned up Hampton, who agreed to tell the court all that he knew about the business, and this presumably, could be much to your advantage.

You will want your barrister to stress these points: that you told Hampton all about it, and about Field's and Dewey's approval, before you were charged with the offence; and that you discussed the whole business in the public house, with Field and Dewey, nearly two weeks before you placed the bet, and that you obtained their consent. You appreciate that their consent does not add up to the consent of the entire committee, since Banforth and Hampton knew nothing about it. Nevertheless, Field and Dewey and yourself add up to a majority.

30 Communicating Without Words

We tend mostly to think of communication as something verbal. Two people say various things to one another, and providing each understands the language used, then a communication successfully takes place. But of course, a great deal of himan communication involves no verbal language at all, and even where we use words, these words represent only part of what is communicated. As an example, consider the way we rely on smiles, posture, gesture, etc., when we meet someone at, say, a party. A friendly look says more than a friendly statement. And sometimes, the look belies the statement.

And so we quite often land in trouble for the way we look, and no amount of denial will help us. Take the following case:

> *'No Smiling' order for accused boy*
> A youth was told to stop smiling when he was charged at West London Magistrates' Court today on two counts of begging.
> He told the court that he needed money for his bus fare home and that he begged for it in the street.
> 'I am very sorry,' the accused said.
> 'You don't look sorry,' replied the Magistrate. 'In fact you are smiling. You obviously think it very funny.'
> The accused replied that he sometimes looked as though he was smiling even when he wasn't. 'It's a handicap,' said the accused.
> The Magistrate said he did not accept the accused's explanation, but would give him a lenient sentence as this was his first offence. He was fined £5 and given two weeks to pay.

Can you think of any occasion when you yourself were 'misunderstood' not because of what you said but because of 'the way you looked' when you said it? What happened?

How easily do misunderstandings like this arise? What causes them?

* * *

Kinesics

A new science has grown up in recent years designed to measure the different ways in which we communicate without words. It is called *kinesics,* and it has already acquired its own rather complicated vocabulary. Its followers have worked out (and given names for)

Kinesics

the different ways in which we nod the head on recognising someone or something, the different types of eyelid movement, of shoulder-shrugging, hand- and arm-movement, and so on. They have found ways too of measuring their intensity and duration. Their aim is to find a means of describing accurately all aspects of our movement.

Here is an example.

First, the simple event:

Just west of Alburquerque on Highway 66 two soldiers stood astride their duffle bags, thumbing a ride. A large car sped by them and the driver jerked his head back, signifying refusal. The two soldiers wheeled and one saluted him while the other thumbed his nose after the retreating car.

And now, the translation of this event into the language of kinesics:

The two soldiers stood in parallel, legs akimbo, with an intrafemoral index of 45 degrees. In unison, each raised his right upper arm to about an 80 degree angle with his body, and with the lower arm at approximately a 100 degree angle, moved the arm in an anterior-posterior sweep with a double pivot at shoulder and elbow; the four fingers of the right hand were curled and the thumb was posteriorly hooked; the right palm faced the body. Their left arms were held closer to the body with an elbow bend of about 90 degrees. The left four fingers were curled and the thumb was partially hidden as it crooked into their respective belts.

The driver of the car focused momentarily on the boys, raised both brows, flared his nostrils, lifted his upper lip, revealed his upper teeth, and with his head cocked, moved it in a posterior-anterior inverted nod which in its backward aspect had about twice the velocity of the movement which returned the head and face to the midline and, thus, to driving focus.

Without apparent hesitation the boys right-stepped posteriorly, one of the boys moving in echo following the movement of the other. Facing the retreating car, one of the boys raised his upper lip to expose his teeth, furrowed his forehead, lowered his eyebrows, contracted the lateral aspect of his orbits, and flared his nostrils. His right arm swept from its posteriorly thrust position on a shoulder pivot, to rest, fist clenched, upper arm across the right half of the body and the lower right arm thrust up and slightly anterior to the body line. The left hand left the belt and the lower arm swept right and upward to meet the descending upper (right) arm. The left hand grasped the right biceps, as, fist still clenched, the right arm moved quickly in an anterior-superior thrust in line with his shoulder and the retreating automobile. . . .

From *Kinesics and Context* by Ray Birdwhistell, Penguin University Books 1971

For discussion

Kinesics tries to describe bodily movements without assuming what is going on inside people's minds. It describes *movements*, not *people's intentions*.

Bearing this in mind:

1 Watch someone performing a simple action, such as waving at a friend, opening the door for someone else, etc.
   Describe the action (not necessarily in any particular jargon) as one would in kinesics.
   Can others make sense of your descriptions? (It should not be calculated to mislead!) Now give a simple, everyday description of what you have been describing.
2 Set up the following brief improvisations, and ask others to look at the scenes without knowing beforehand what they are looking at. Ask them to make written notes describing clearly what they see. Again, ask them *not* to describe what they think is in the actors' minds, but to restrict themselves to what they actually can see.

   Two people meet while going about their work; they know each other well, but do not have time to speak; they expect to see each other again soon; they are both in a hurry.

   Two people meet; they pass each other; then they both realise they have met before; they turn back; they are about to speak; they realise they are mistaken; they pass on.

   X brings a letter for Y; Y takes the letter without comment; X waits for a reply; there is no reply; X waits for a tip; there is no tip; when he cannot be seen by Y, X makes a rude face at him and goes; Y carries on reading the letter.

   Is it possible to describe such events without assuming *what people think they are actually doing?*
3 Think of a situation in which people have to communicate without at that moment being able to speak. Improvise the story.
4 Think of a situation in which people's 'kinesic' behaviour repeatedly contradicts what they are saying — as when you show annoyance at meeting someone you profess to be delighted to meet.
5 'All professions and occupations have their own kind of non-verbal ways of behaving, and we recognise them accordingly'. How true is this? Consider it in relation, for example, to policemen, teachers, friends, soccer players, bullies, etc.
6 To what extent do we judge people by their gestures and movement? Can these be misleading? Devise and improvise a situation in which people to some extent misunderstand each other because of the unspoken messages that they 'send across'.

For Further Reference

Books and articles I have found useful:

The relationship of drama and imagination

Eric Bentley, *The Playwright as Thinker*, Harcourt Brace, NY 1967
Richard Courtney, *Play, Drama and Thought*, Pitman 1974
S Eisenstein, *Film Form*, Harcourt Brace 1949
Ruth Griffiths, *Language and Imagination in Early Childhood*, Kegan Paul 1935
D W Harding, *Experience into Words*, Penguin University Books 1973
Marjorie Hourd, *The Education of the Poetic Spirit*, Heinemann 1949
J Moffett, *Drama: What is Happening*, National Council of Teachers of English, Chicago 1967
Newcastle University, Institute of Education, *Achievements in Teaching: The Privilege of Language* 1967
C Stanislavsky, *An Actor Prepares*, Penguin 1967
D W Winnicott, *Playing and Reality*, Tavistock 1971

On teaching improvised drama

David Adland, *The Group Approach to Drama*, Longman 1964-72
John Allen, Drama (*Education Survey* 2) HMSO 1967
Gabriel Barnfield, *Creative Drama in Schools*, Macmillan 1970
Derek Bowskill, *Acting and Stagecraft Made Simple*, W H Allen 1973
Bullock Report, *A Language for Life*, Chapter 10, HMSO 1975
John Challen, *Drama Casebook*, Methuen, 1973
Brian Clark, *Group Theatre*, Pitman 1972
David Clegg, *'Improvisation in education'* article for Theatre Quarterly, January 1973, also the following issue for correspondence following the article
P A Coggin, *Drama and Education*, Thames and Hudson 1967
C Cook, *The Play Way*, Heinemann 1917
Christopher Day, *Drama for the Middle and Upper School*, Batsford 1975
Alec Davison, contribution to *'Language and Literacy in our Schools'*, edited by Harold Rosen, University of London Institute of Education 1975

N Dodd, editor, *Drama and Theatre in Education,* Faber 1971 (see especially, articles by Gavin Bolton and Dorothy Heathcote)
Gerard Gould, *Dramatic Involvement,* Blackwell 1970
Joan Haggerty, *Please, Miss, Can I Play God?* Methuen 1966
Dorothy Heathcote, *Improvisation* in 'English in Education', Vol 1, No. 3
Albert Hunt, *Hopes for Great Happenings,* Eyre Methuen 1976
John Hodgson & Ernest Richards, *Improvisation,* Methuen 1972
Sue Jennings, *Remedial Drama,* Pitman 1972
Colin King, *A Space on the Floor,* Ward Lock 1972
Mike Leigh, interviewed by Sheridan Morley in *The Times* 15 July 1977
David Male, *Approaches to Drama,* Unwin 1973
William Martin & Gordon Vallins, *Exploration Drama,* Evans 1968
Lynn McGregor, *Developments in Drama Teaching,* Open Books 1976
Lynn McGregor, Kenneth Robinson, Schools Council Drama Project 1977
Cecily O'Neill and others, *Drama Guidelines,* Heinemann 1976
John O'Toole, *Theatre in Education,* Hodder and Stoughton 1976
R N Pemberton-Billing & J D Clegg, *Teaching Drama,* University of London 1968
Kenneth Pickering, Bill Horrocks & David Male *Investigating Drama,* Allen & Unwin 1974
Anna Scher, *First Act Drama Kit,* Ward Lock 1976
John Seely, *In Context: Language and Drama in the Secondary School,* Oxford University Press 1976
David Self, *Teaching Practical Drama,* Collins 1976
Peter Slade, *An Introduction to Child Drama,* University of London 1969
Viola Spolin, *Improvisation for the Theatre,* Northwestern University Press 1963
Rex Walford and J L Taylor, *Simulation in the Classroom,* Penguin 1972
Brenda Walker, *Teaching Creative Drama,* Batsford 1970
Brian Way, *Development Through Drama,* Longman 1967

Magazines and Journals with particular interest in improvised drama:

Amateur Stage (published from 1, Hawthorne Road, Hayes, Bromley, Kent)
Creative Drama (Education Drama Association, Drama Centre, Rea Street, Birmingham 5)
Drama (British Theatre Association, 9 Fitzroy Square, W.1)
Speech and Drama (Society of Teachers of Speech and Drama, editor — 3 Arran Mews, Canterbury CT1 1JA)
Theatre Quarterly (ABP Ltd., North Way, Andover, Hants.)
Young Drama (PO Box 2, Stroud, Gloucs.)